THE ULTIMATE
GUIDE FOR
E-COMMERCE

*Ignite your E-Commerce Empire, Conquer the Market, and
Command Essential Strategies for Phenomenal Growth*

by

Author: Dr.Rekha Rani Chauhan

Arushee Tomar

PREFACE

Welcome to the exciting world of e-commerce! In an age where the digital realm is increasingly intertwined with our daily lives, the opportunities and challenges presented by online retail are more significant than ever before. This book is guide you to navigating this dynamic landscape.

E-commerce has evolved from its humble beginnings into a global powerhouse, reshaping the way we shop, do business, and interact with the marketplace. Whether you're a seasoned entrepreneur, a budding e-commerce enthusiast, or simply someone curious about the workings of online retail, this book is designed to equip you with the knowledge and tools necessary to succeed in this ever-evolving field.

Throughout these pages, we will delve into the intricacies of e-commerce, from understanding the fundamental concepts and technologies to exploring the nuances of e-commerce strategy, marketing, and logistics. The digital marketplace is vast and diverse, and our journey together will encompass everything from launching an e-commerce business to optimizing its performance and adapting to emerging trends.

In the following chapters, you will find a wealth of insights, practical advice, and real-world examples to help you thrive in the world of e-commerce. We aim to demystify the complexities of online retail, providing you with a comprehensive resource that empowers you to make informed decisions, overcome challenges, and seize the boundless opportunities that e-commerce offers.

This book is a product of extensive research and practical experience, and it is our hope that it will serve as a valuable resource on your e-commerce journey.

Whether you are a business professional seeking to expand your online presence, an aspiring e-commerce entrepreneur, or a curious reader intrigued by the workings of the digital marketplace and the students of MBA, B.Com, B.B.A, B.C.A and Vocational Course E-Commerce. We invite you to embark on this adventure with us.

So, let's dive into the world of e-commerce and discover the tools and knowledge you need to thrive in this dynamic and ever-evolving realm.

TABLE OF CONTENTS

CHAPTER 1: INTRODUCTION TO E-COMMERCE

"The success of e-commerce lies in understanding customer needs and exceeding their expectations. "

- Steve Jobs

1.1. Introduction

We're currently in the e-century, where the Internet and information and communications technologies (ICT) play a crucial role in economic growth and productivity. Internet-based technologies and networks have the potential to boost productivity, cut costs, and create new market opportunities. Nowadays, it's not uncommon to use the Internet and email for business transactions. However, a lack of technical and management skills in Information and Communications Technology poses a challenge.

Fortunately, there's a wide array of resources to help improve your e-commerce skills. Identify the skills you need and find the right resources to build them. These skills can range from basic abilities like word processing and internet navigation to more advanced capabilities such as designing websites and managing databases. Various resources, including online platforms, books, magazines, seminars, and training courses, are available to enhance your understanding of the e-commerce environment and develop your technical skills. With this in mind, a summary of the background of Electronic Commerce is provided.

1.2. Meaning and Definition of E-Commerce

E-Commerce, short for Electronics Commerce, represents a modern business approach that caters to the needs of business organizations, vendors, and customers aiming to reduce costs, enhance the quality of goods and services, and expedite delivery. It involves the paperless exchange of business information through various methods, including

- Electronic Data Exchange (EDI)

- Electronic Mail (e-mail)

- Electronic Bulletin Boards

- Electronic Fund Transfer (EFT)

- Other network-based technologies.

The essence of e-commerce lies in leveraging the internet to conduct business more efficiently and swiftly. It encompasses the process of buying and selling over the Internet or any transaction involving the transfer of ownership or rights to use goods or services through a computer-mediated network, eliminating the need for paper documents.

Electronic commerce or e-commerce refers to a wide range of online business activities for products and services. It also pertains to "any form of business transaction in which the parties interact electronically rather than by physical exchanges or direct physical contact." It involves various electronic tools like computers, telephones, fax machines, barcode readers, credit cards, automated teller machines (ATM), or other electronic devices, without relying on paper-based documents. E-commerce covers procurement, order entry, transaction processing, payment authentication, inventory control, and customer support.

Categorically, e-commerce is divided into three segments: business-to-business (B2B), business-to-consumer (B2C), and consumer-to-consumer (C2C), also known as electronic commerce. It refers to conducting business over the Internet using applications like e-mail, instant messaging, shopping carts, Web services, UDDI, FTP, and EDI. E-commerce serves as a business model or segment allowing firms or individuals to engage in electronic network transactions, primarily over the Internet. It operates across four major market segments: business-to-business, business-to-consumer, consumer-to-consumer, and consumer-to-business. By providing a more cost-effective and efficient distribution chain, e-commerce has enabled firms to establish or enhance their market presence.

E-Commerce Definitions

The concept of e-commerce encompasses various business activities, including business-to-business (B2B), business-to-consumer (B2C), extended enterprise computing (referred to as "newly emerging value chains"), d-commerce, and m-commerce. E-commerce constitutes a subset of e-business, specifically focusing on the trading component of electronic business. While there are multiple definitions and explanations of e-commerce, the following definition offers a clear distinction. Numerous interpretations and perspectives exist regarding e-commerce, outlined as follows:

- According to Vladimir Zwass, editor-in-chief of the International Journal of Electronic Commerce, electronic commerce is sharing business information, maintaining business relationships, and conducting business transactions by means of telecommunications networks.

- Electronic Commerce is where business transactions take place via telecommunications networks, especially the Internet – E. Turban, J. Lee, D. King and H.M. Chung,

- Electronic commerce is about doing business electronically – P. Timers

- It pertains to "any form of business transaction in which the parties interact electronically rather than by physical exchanges or direct physical contact." – MK, Euro Info Correspondence Centre (Belgrade, Serbia),

- E-commerce is usually associated with buying and selling over the Internet or conducting any transaction involving the transfer of ownership or rights to use goods or services through a computer-mediated network. – Thomas L. Massenburg

- A complete definition is: E-commerce is the use of electronic communications and digital information processing technology in business transactions to create, transform, and redefine relationships for value creation between or among organizations and between organizations and individuals. – Emmanuel Lallana, Rudy Quimbo, Zorayda Ruth Andam, ePrimer.

From your reading, it should be apparent to you that electronic commerce is more than online shopping.

1.3. The Difference between E-Commerce and e-business

There exists a debate among consultants and academics regarding the interpretation and constraints of both e-commerce and e-business. Some contend that e-commerce encompasses the entire realm of electronically-based organizational activities supporting a firm's market exchanges, including the complete information system infrastructure. Conversely, others argue that e-business encompasses the entire scope of internal and external electronically-based activities, encompassing e-commerce as well.

The term e-business is primarily used to denote the digital enablement of transactions and processes within a firm involving information systems under the firm's control. In our perspective, e-business generally excludes commercial transactions involving the exchange of value across organizational boundaries. For instance, a company's online inventory control mechanisms fall under the umbrella of e-business. Still, these internal processes don't directly generate revenue from external businesses or consumers, as e-commerce inherently does. Nevertheless, it's acknowledged that a firm's e-business infrastructure supports online e-commerce exchanges, sharing similar infrastructure and skill sets in both e-business and e-commerce.

The distinction between e-commerce and e-business systems becomes less clear at the business firm boundary, specifically where internal business systems connect with suppliers or customers. E-business applications transition into e-commerce precisely when an exchange of value takes place.

1.4. Functions of E-Commerce

The following are five functions you should be doing daily in your e-commerce business.

1.4.1. Search Engine Optimization (SEO)

- **Unique Relevant Content:**

  1. Google values uniqueness and relevance.

  2. Content should align with the site's theme.

  3. Use good keywords related to the site's focus.

- **Header Tags (H1 and H2):**

  1. Each page should have an H1 tag indicating the main focus.

  2. H2 tags can be used for other important page sections.

- **Optimized Page Titles:**

  1. Include keywords in page titles.

  2. Enhances search engine visibility and alignment with the focus.

- **Internal Linking:**

  1. Link keywords in unique content to related pages.

  2. Significant for overall website strength and user navigation.

- **Friendly URLs:**

  1. Structure URLs with related phrases.

  2. Example: http://www.zobristinc.com/our_solutions/eZ_Commerce/.

  3. Enhances user experience and search engine optimization.

1.4.2. Selecting New Products

- Focus on offering what the customer is interested in purchasing rather than pushing products you want to sell. This is a prevalent mistake, particularly when there's a tempting price for a specific product. However, if there's no demand for that product, the pricing becomes irrelevant.

- Identify customer preferences. Understand your value proposition for the products you offer and leverage your niche market.

1.4.3. Merchandising New Productions

- Emphasize the importance of high-quality images for your products.

- Utilize hero photos on category pages, showcasing best-selling products prominently.

- Highlight and promote the latest releases in newsletters and display them prominently in categories or on your homepage.

- Target marketing efforts towards customers who have previously purchased related items.

1.4.4. Customer Service

- Prioritize customer satisfaction.

- Ensure timely delivery of orders.

- Maintain order accuracy.

- Promptly reship in cases of delivery failure, damage, or missing parts.

- Avoid cutting corners on every order; occasional losses may be necessary to prioritize customer happiness and secure their loyalty for future orders.

1.4.5. Monitoring your KPIs / Analytics

- Keep a close eye on your analytics reports to identify top-selling items and prioritize them in product listings for easier customer access. For those using IBM WebSphere Commerce, consider leveraging our Smart Merchandiser product, offering analytic overlays on each product in every category to aid in intelligent merchandising decisions.

- Address cart abandonment issues by remarketing products to customers using their email addresses. Please encourage them to complete their checkout within a specified timeframe by providing incentives.

1.5. Opportunities and challenges in e-commerce

E-commerce has become a crucial component of India's trade facilitation policy. Since 1991, when explicit economic reforms were implemented, the emphasis on streamlining international trade through both policy and procedural reforms has been integral to

13

India's trade and fiscal strategies. This has led to a technological revolution marked by widespread adoption of the Internet, web technologies, and their applications. The impact of E-Commerce on global business practices has evolved significantly and continues to reshape the way business is conducted worldwide.

1.5.1. Opportunities

Businesses in India are becoming more aware of the opportunities provided by e-commerce. E-commerce offers a new space for connecting with consumers and carrying out transactions. Virtual stores operate round the clock, providing a continuous platform for businesses to engage with their customers.

- **Global Trade**

E-business stands out as a significant contributor to the globalization of business, alongside other influential factors such as a reduction in trade barriers and the globalization of capital markets. The e-business sector in India has witnessed substantial growth, with a compounded annual growth rate of 30% since FY09. Projections indicate that it is poised to become a substantial $18 billion (approximately Rs 1,116,00 crore) opportunity by FY15.

- **Virtual Businesses**

Business firms can now transform into virtual E-businesses. Virtual business leverages electronic methods for conducting transactions instead of relying on traditional face-to-face interactions.

- **Lower search costs**

The Internet reduces search costs and enhances price transparency. E-business has demonstrated its cost-effectiveness for businesses by minimizing expenses related to marketing, processing, inventory management, customer care, and more.

- **Round the clock**

Customers can conduct transactions for a product or inquire about any products/services offered by a company at any time, from any place, regardless of their location.

1.5.2. Challenges

The surge in e-commerce activity in India has captured global interest. Despite lower per-capita purchasing power, the sheer size of the population makes India a compelling emerging market for e-commerce. However, navigating the Indian market is not without its hurdles. Here are the eight key challenges that e-commerce businesses encounter in India.

- **Indian customers return much of the merchandise they purchase online.**

A significant number of commodities purchased online by Indian customers end up being returned. E-business in India attracts many first-time buyers, indicating uncertainty about what to anticipate from e-business websites. Consequently, buyers may need to avoid aggressive sales tactics, only to regret their decision upon actual product delivery, leading to returns. Returns pose challenges for e-business companies, particularly in terms of reverse logistics, and this complexity intensifies in the context of cross-border e-business.

- **Cash on delivery is the preferred payment mode.**

Cash on delivery is the preferred payment mode. Low credit card access and low trust in online transactions have led to cash on delivery being the preferred payment choice in India. Compared to electronic payments, manual cash collection is thorough, risky, and expensive.

- **Payment gateways have a high failure rate.**

Indian payment gateways experience a higher-than-usual failure rate compared to global standards. E-business companies relying on Indian payment gateways are facing a loss of business, as numerous customers opt not to retry making payments after a transaction failure.

- **Internet penetration is low.**

Internet penetration remains low, with India's current levels significantly below those in many Western countries. Additionally, the quality of connectivity could be better in several regions. However, both these issues are on the verge of resolution. The day is not far when connectivity challenges will no longer be prominent on the list of obstacles facing e-business in India.

- **Feature phones still rule the roost.**

While the total number of mobile phone users in India is substantial, a significant majority still utilizes feature phones rather than smartphones. Consequently, this consumer group needs help in making e-business purchases while on the move. Although it may take a couple of more years for India to witness a shift in Favor of smartphones, the rapid decrease in the price of entry-level smartphones is an encouraging sign.

- **Postal addresses are not standardized.**

In India, when an online order is placed, it is common to receive a call from the logistics company to inquire about the exact location. This is attributed to the need for more standardization in the way postal addresses are written, where merely providing an address may need to be clarified.

- **Logistics is a problem in thousands of Indian towns.**

Due to the vast size of the country, numerous towns pose challenges to accessibility. The logistics issue is further complicated by the prevalent preference for cash on delivery as the payment option in India. Various stakeholders, including international logistics providers, private Indian companies, and government-owned postal services, are making commendable efforts to address and resolve these logistical challenges.

- **Overfunded competitors are driving up the cost of customer acquisition**

The prospects for e-commerce companies in the long term are so compelling that some investors are willing to spend disproportionately high amounts of money to acquire market share today. Consequently, the Indian consumer benefits from a wealth of choices in this competitive environment.

1.6. Future Scope and Growth

The growth of e-commerce will be driven by two factors: firstly, changes in macroeconomic parameters such as disposable income, internet penetration, and the influx of investments, and secondly, segment-specific factors that influence the industry.

- **Macro-economic factors**

1. Personal Disposable Income will continue to rise.

According to the International Monetary Fund (IMF), personal disposable income will rise; it signals that the purchasing power of the people and their standard of living has increased. As a result, demand for goods and services is expected to rise. With more disposable income, the benefits of time-saving offered by e-commerce will lead to growth in the sector.

2. The number of active Internet users in India is poised to rise.

Internet penetration has experienced a Compound Annual Growth Rate (CAGR) of 30% since 2007. The expansion of the internet user base is anticipated to persist, leading to a surge in digital media advertisements. As advertising increases, both the trial rate and repeat rate for online retailing are expected to rise. This surge is likely to catalyze growth in both the travel and non-travel segments, driven by increased customer acquisition.

3. Demand for debit and credit cards will see a rise.

The demand for debit and credit cards has also seen a steady rise over the last few years. Most of the banks now provide online banking and debit card facilities with every new account. With the financial inclusion drive by the RBI, the number of bank accounts (and hence the number of debit cards) will definitely see a rise. This, coupled with rising disposable income, will invariably lead to more online transactions.

- **Segment Specific factors**

In the online travel segment, the growth of the tourism industry and the increasing demand for domestic travel will have positive externalities on the e-commerce industry. Travel websites, expanding their offerings to include features like hotel booking and package tours, contribute to the convenience factor, fostering growth. Moreover, the Internet provides users with the choice to evaluate offers, compare prices, and select options that align with their demands.

In the online retail space, the absence of showrooms and the high cost of transportation create barriers to accessing global brands for those in tier 2 cities, thereby amplifying the demand for online shopping.

1.7. Summary

There needs to be a universally agreed-upon definition of E-Commerce. Its impact extends to three major stakeholders: society, organizations, and customers. E-Commerce brings forth several advantages, including cost savings, heightened efficiency, customization, and access to global marketplaces. However, it also presents limitations affecting each stakeholder, such as information overload, reliability and security concerns, access costs, social divisions, and challenges in internet policing.

To enhance the general understanding of E-Commerce, various frameworks have been introduced to examine it from diverse perspectives. These frameworks aid in identifying the components of E-Commerce and provide businesses with a better understanding of its practical applicability.

CHAPTER 2: MODELS OF E-COMMERCE

"In the digital era, e-commerce success is not just about selling products; it's about creating memorable experiences for your customers."

- Jeff Bezos.

An e-business model refers to the strategy a company adopts to achieve profitability on the Internet.

Various buzzwords are used to describe different aspects of electronic business, and there are subgroups like content providers, auction sites, and pure-play Internet retailers, especially in the business-to-consumer space.

E-commerce, short for Electronic Commerce, encompasses several business models, and they can be broadly categorized into the following types:

- Business - to - Business (B2B)
- Business-to-consumer (B2C)
- Consumer - to - Consumer (C2C)
- Consumer-to-Business (C2B)
- Business - to - Government (B2G)
- Government-to-Business (G2B)

2.1. Business-to-Business (B2B)

Business-to-business (B2B) refers to a type of commerce transaction that occurs between businesses, such as interactions between a manufacturer and a wholesaler or between a wholesaler and a retailer.

In the B2B model, business is conducted between companies rather than directly with individual consumers. This is different from the

Business-to-Consumer (B2C) and Business-to-Government (B2G) models.

In a B2B transaction, a website following this business model sells its products to an intermediate buyer, who then sells the product to the final customer.

For instance, a wholesaler may place an order on a company's website, receive the consignment, and then sell the end product to the final customer at their retail outlet.

Key points about B2B transactions:

- **Both Parties are Businesses**: In B2B transactions, both the seller and the buyer are business entities.

- **Intermediaries in the Process**: The model often involves intermediaries such as wholesalers, distributors, and retailers.

- **Relationship Building:** B2B transactions cover a wide range of applications that facilitate businesses in forming relationships with distributors, resellers, suppliers, and other entities.

Examples of companies following the B2B model include IBM, Hewlett-Packard (HP), CISCO, and Dell.

Online platforms like Chemconnect.com and chemdex.com are also examples of B2B platforms that bring together two firms in a virtual market, facilitating transactions and collaborations between businesses.

B2B applications are prevalent in various areas, showcasing their significance in facilitating business transactions and relationships.

Here are some key areas where B2B applications can be witnessed:

- **Supplier Management**

    1. B2B applications assist in managing relationships with suppliers.

    2. Streamlining communication, order placements, and tracking deliveries are common functionalities.

- **Inventory Management**

    1. B2B systems help businesses effectively manage their inventory.

    2. This includes tracking stock levels, reordering processes, and ensuring timely availability of products.

- **Distribution Management**

    1. B2B applications play a crucial role in managing the distribution of goods.

    2. They help optimize logistics, track shipments, and coordinate with various distribution channels.

- **Channel Management**

    1. B2B applications facilitate the management of distribution channels.

    2. This involves overseeing relationships with intermediaries such as wholesalers, retailers, and agents.

- **Payment Management**

    1. B2B systems streamline the payment process between businesses.

2. They often include features for invoicing, billing, and electronic payment methods, enhancing efficiency in financial transactions.

Diagrammatic Representation of the B2B Model

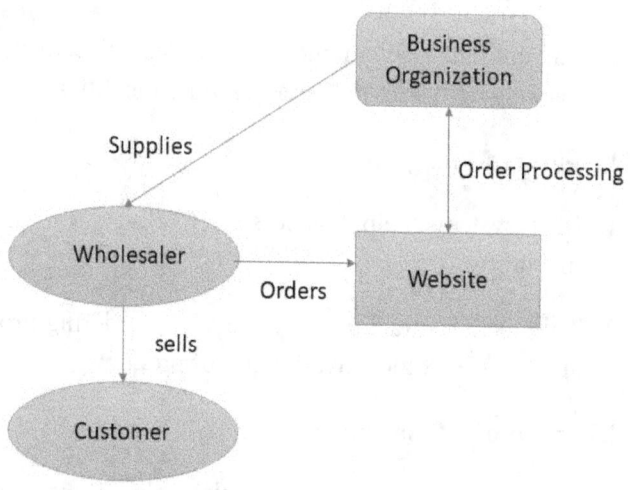

Models in B2B

The B2B model can be supplier-centric, buyer-centric, or intermediary-centric models.

- **Supplier-Centric Model:** In this Model, the electronic commerce marketplace is initiated and operated by a dominant supplier. Customers engage with the supplier on its platform, and the supplier may offer tailored solutions and pricing to meet buyer needs. Intel and Cisco exemplify companies adopting this model.

- **Buyer-Centric Model:** This Model involves large business organizations with significant purchasing capabilities establishing and managing the electronic commerce marketplace. Buyers utilize this platform to request quotations and oversee the entire purchase process. The US government and the General Electric Trading Process Network serve as examples of the buyer-centric model.

- **Intermediary-Centric Model:** In this Model, a third party takes the lead in establishing and overseeing the electronic commerce marketplace. This intermediary attracts both buyers and sellers to engage with each other on its platform. The buyer initiates requests, sellers respond, and the intermediary facilitates interactions until a final decision is reached in the purchase or sale of goods.

Advantages of B2B

Selling products to businesses through an online channel, as seen in the B2B model, comes with unique advantages:

- **Instant Purchases:** Online platforms enable swift transactions, allowing companies to establish contact, make initial transactions, and set up ongoing systems. This not only facilitates frequent purchases but also often leads to cost savings.

- **Increased Revenue:** The availability of 24/7 online ordering breaks down time zone barriers, enabling companies to cater to clients in different parts of the world. This continuous accessibility contributes to a significant increase in revenue.

- **Expanded Company Presence:** Embracing the online community enhances a company's visibility and brand awareness. As people increasingly turn to the internet for various needs, having an online presence ensures that potential clients can easily find and engage with the company.

- **Closer Business Relationships:** Conducting business with other companies online fosters closer relationships. Despite the absence of face-to-face interactions, frequent online transactions contribute to the development of stronger connections between businesses.

Disadvantages of B2B

Embracing a B2B model can offer significant profits through the sale of high-cost products or bulk orders.

Still, it comes with distinct disadvantages that diverge from standard business-to-consumer practices:

- **Limited Market:** Selling to other businesses means dealing with a smaller buying group compared to businesses targeting consumers. The number of prospective buyers is limited, often in the thousands, making each lead and existing customer highly valuable. Losing a single large customer can significantly impact the bottom line.

- **Long Purchase Decision Time:** B2B sales involve a complex decision-making process with multiple stakeholders, resulting in extended decision times, sometimes spanning months. Unlike consumer purchases that typically involve one or two decision-makers and shorter decision times, B2B sellers must navigate lengthier cycles.

- **Inverted Power Structure:** In B2B transactions, buyers hold more power than sellers. They can demand customizations, set exacting specifications, and negotiate pricing aggressively, given the seller's heavier reliance on retaining customers. This necessitates a high level of flexibility from B2B sellers in product development and production.

- **Sales Process:** The B2B sales process requires substantial face time, often involving multiple meetings driven by quantifiable factors rather than emotional considerations.

Success in B2B sales hinges on the salesperson's ability to demonstrate product functionality, propose modifications addressing specific buyer problems, and ensure a solid return on investment.

2.2. Business-to-Consumer (B2C)

The B2C model, short for Business-to-Consumer, involves the direct interaction between businesses and individual consumers through the Internet. In this model, businesses sell their products directly to end consumers. A typical B2C transaction occurs when a customer visits a business's website, views the available products, selects an item, and places an order. The website then notifies the business organization via email, and the organization dispatches the ordered product to the customer. B2C is also referred to as internet retailing or E-tailing.

Range of Transactions: B2C encompasses various transactions, including electronic shopping, information searches (e.g., for railway timetables), and interactive games delivered over the Internet.

Popular Items: Products commonly sold using the B2C model include airline tickets, books, computers, videotapes, music CDs, toys, health and beauty products, jewelry, and more.

Key Features:

- **Heavy Advertising**: B2C businesses often require significant advertising efforts to attract a large number of customers. This is crucial for driving consumer traffic to their online platforms.

- **High Investment:** There is a substantial investment in terms of hardware and software infrastructure to support the online sales platform and ensure a seamless shopping experience.

- **Customer Care Service:** Providing strong customer support is essential in the B2C model. Offering excellent customer service ensures customer satisfaction, loyalty, and a positive brand image.

In the B2C e-commerce model, the consumer shopping procedure involves a series of steps:

- The consumer begins by determining their specific requirements, such as the product or service they are looking to purchase.

- They then explore the website's offerings to find items that meet their requirements.

- After identifying potential items, the consumer compares them based on various factors like price, delivery date, and product specifications.

- Once a decision is made, the consumer proceeds to place an order for the selected product or service. This typically involves adding the item to the shopping cart and following the website's order process.

- The next step is completing the transaction by providing payment information. This can include credit/debit card details, digital wallet information, or other accepted payment methods.

- After confirming the order and making the payment, the consumer waits for the delivery of the purchased item. The business organization is responsible for dispatching the product to the specified address.

- Upon receiving the delivered item, the consumer has the opportunity to review and inspect it. This step allows them to ensure that the received product meets their expectations in terms of quality and specifications.

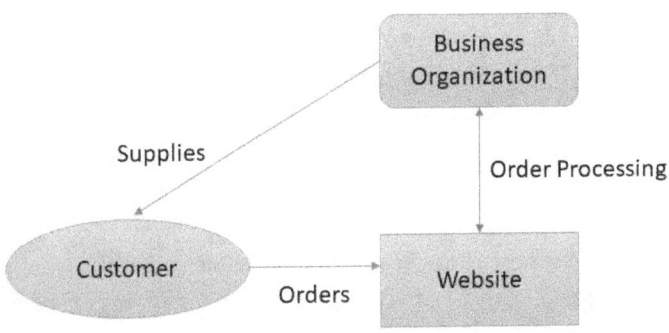

Advantages of E-Commerce for B2C

Businesses: The benefits of B2C e-commerce can be considered either from the viewpoint of the consumer or from that of the business.

From the consumer's perspective, online shopping brings about several advantages:

- **Access to Goods and Services:** Consumers can conveniently explore and purchase a diverse range of goods and services without leaving their homes or other remote locations.

- **Potential for Cost Savings:** Online shopping often presents the possibility of lower costs for products and services compared to traditional brick-and-mortar stores. This is often attributed to reduced overhead expenses for online businesses.

- **Greater Variety of Offerings:** Online platforms offer consumers access to a wide variety of goods and services, providing a broader selection than what may be available in local stores.

- **24/7 Shopping Availability:** The flexibility of online shopping allows consumers to make purchases at any time of the day, offering a level of convenience often described as "the mall that never sleeps."

- **Wide Range of Choices:** Consumers have an abundance of choices when shopping online. They can find and purchase a broad spectrum of items, from airline tickets and groceries to clothing and medicine.

- **Hassle-Free Shopping Experience:** Online shopping eliminates the need to contend with annoying salespeople, navigate crowded shopping malls, or travel to multiple locations to find specific items. It provides a hassle-free and comfortable shopping experience.

From a business perspective, engaging in online commerce provides various benefits:

- **Lower Transaction Costs:** Online sales generally involve lower transaction costs for businesses compared to traditional brick-and-mortar transactions. This can contribute to increased profit margins.

- **Access to Global Markets:** Online platforms offer businesses the opportunity to tap into global markets, providing access to a broader customer base and potentially increasing sales.

- **Global Market Reach:** Businesses can reach a worldwide market with the potential for an unlimited volume of customers. This expansive reach goes beyond geographical limitations, enabling broader market penetration.

- **Cost-Effective Display of Information:** Online platforms allow businesses to showcase information, pictures, and prices of their products or services without the need for extensive investments in colorful advertisements. This cost-effective approach enhances visibility.

- **Streamlined Order Processing:** In some cases, online commerce simplifies the order processing task for businesses. Automated systems can streamline and optimize the handling of orders, making the process more efficient.

- **Reduced Overhead:** Online businesses can operate with decreased, minimal, or even no physical overhead compared to traditional brick-and-mortar establishments. This can lead to significant cost savings in terms of rent, utilities, and other operational expenses.

Disadvantages of B2B:

- **Intense Competition:** The online marketplace is highly competitive, with numerous options for customers to purchase the same product from various sources. This saturation can make it challenging for businesses to stand out.

- **Technology Issues:** Technical problems can arise, affecting the proper functioning of the website. This can result in a loss of customers and potential sales if the site experiences disruptions or difficulties in navigation.

- **Catalog Inflexibility:** The online catalog may need regeneration every time new information or items are added, which can be a cumbersome process and may lead to delays in updating product listings.

- **Limited Market Reach:** B2C businesses may find that their customer base is typically local and confined to a specific geographic area, limiting the potential market reach compared to businesses with a physical presence.

- **Extended Sales Cycle:** B2C transactions often require numerous phone calls and mailings, lengthening the sales cycle and potentially causing delays in closing deals.

- **Higher Cost of Doing Business:** E-commerce operations may incur higher costs, including inventory management, employee expenses, purchasing costs, and order-processing costs associated with traditional methods like faxing, phone calls, and data entry.

- **Inefficient Business Administration:** Administrative tasks, such as updating store inventory levels and shipping logs, might need manual categorization and updates. This manual process can lead to outdated information and inefficiencies.

- **Need for Staffing:** E-commerce businesses often require additional staffing for customer service and sales support services, increasing operational costs.

Disadvantages for the consumer:

- **Security Concerns:** Security issues, especially regarding credit card information, are a primary reason why some people hesitate to make online purchases. Consumers are cautious about sharing sensitive financial information online due to the potential for scams, frauds, and online rip-offs.

- **Customer Service Challenges:** Online consumers may encounter dissatisfaction with their purchases, and addressing concerns or seeking assistance may be more challenging compared to in-person transactions. The absence of face-to-face interaction can lead to perceived difficulties in obtaining adequate customer support for issues such as product queries or returns.

2.3. Consumer-to-Consumer (C2C)

Customer-to-customer (C2C), or Consumer-to-Consumer, e-commerce involves electronic transactions facilitated between individuals, often with the assistance of a third-party platform. An example of C2C is online auctions, exemplified by platforms like eBay. Here, an individual can list items for sale, and others can bid to purchase them. Auction sites typically charge sellers a commission for using their services, acting as intermediaries connecting buyers and sellers. While they try to prevent the sale of illegal goods, they have limited control over product quality.

Websites following the C2C business model provide a platform for consumers to sell assets such as residential property, cars, motorcycles, or rent rooms by publishing information on the site. These platforms may or may not charge consumers for their services. Interested buyers can view posts or advertisements on the website and choose to purchase the product or service from the initial consumer.

Online classified advertising sites, like Craigslist and Gumtree, are popular areas for C2C transactions. Even major online retailers such as Amazon allow individuals to sell products through their platforms. C2C e-commerce fosters a direct connection between consumers, enabling them to buy and sell a wide range of goods and services in a virtual marketplace.

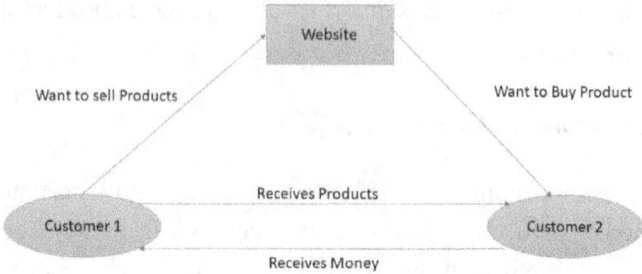

The future of C2C e-commerce is anticipated to witness growth due to its cost-minimizing nature by eliminating the need for extensive third-party involvement. However, several challenges persist, including the need for robust quality control mechanisms and payment guarantees. Additionally, difficulties may arise in making credit card payments.

Key features and aspects of C2C transactions include:

- **Dual Role for Customers:** The same customer can function as both a buyer and a seller within the C2C framework, showcasing the versatility of this model.

- **Advanced Online Marketplaces:** Online marketplaces offer advanced features, allowing buyers to browse products based on various criteria such as best-sellers, popularity, or locality.

- **Dynamic Bidding System:** Different sellers can bid on products listed by buyers, creating a dynamic bidding system. This allows buyers to receive diverse price offers and incentives from various sellers.

- **Social Media Integration:** Social media linking functionalities are integrated, incorporating community or forum discussions and links to blogs and other social media platforms. This enhances user engagement and interaction.

- **Back-End Administration Interface:** The back-end interface provides features for administration to manage buyer and seller accounts, payment settings, gallery settings, and other administrative functions. This ensures the smooth functioning and oversight of the C2C platform.

Advantages of Customer-to-Customer (C2C)

- **24/7 Availability:** C2C platforms are accessible round the clock, providing consumers the flexibility to engage in shopping whenever they desire.

- **Regular Website Updating:** Websites facilitating C2C transactions are regularly updated, ensuring that consumers have access to the latest information and offerings.

- **Higher Profitability for Consumers:** Consumers selling products to other consumers benefit from higher profitability by eliminating intermediaries. Direct transactions between consumers often lead to better profit margins.

- **Low Transaction Costs:** C2C e-commerce involves low transaction costs. Sellers can showcase their goods online at a more cost-effective rate compared to the expenses associated with renting physical retail space.

- **Direct Communication:** Consumers can directly communicate with sellers without the need for intermediaries. This direct interaction fosters a personalized and efficient buying and selling experience.

Disadvantages of Customer-to-Customer (C2C)

- **Unsecured Payments:** Payments made in C2C transactions lack guarantees, posing a risk for both buyers and sellers. There may be concerns regarding the security of financial transactions.

- **Potential for Scams and Theft:** Scammers may attempt to create fraudulent websites mimicking well-known C2C platforms like eBay. This could lead to theft or deception, as unsuspecting customers may be drawn to these fake sites.

- **Quality Control Challenges:** C2C platforms often face challenges in controlling the quality of products being sold. The absence of stringent quality control measures may result in variations in product quality and reliability.

2.4. Consumer-to-Business (C2B)

Consumer-to-business (C2B), also known as Customer-to-Business, represents a relatively recent e-commerce model where individual customers take the initiative to offer products and services to companies willing to purchase them. This model stands in contrast to the traditional Business-to-Consumer (B2C) approach.

In the C2B model, customers actively reach out to enterprises through the Internet, presenting questions, suggestions, and ideas that can be valuable for product or service innovation. Enterprises can facilitate the C2B model by incorporating discussion forums on their websites or social network pages, often leveraging word-of-mouth marketing.

In the C2B framework, a consumer initiates contact with a website that features multiple business organizations providing a specific service. The consumer indicates the amount they are willing to spend on the service. For instance, a consumer might compare interest rates on personal loans or car loans offered by various banks through a website. A business organization that can fulfill the consumer's requirements within the specified budget approaches the customer and offers its services.

Early platforms like Elance pioneered this type of transaction, enabling sellers to showcase their skills and allowing prospective buyers to advertise projects. Similar sites, including People per Hour and Guru, operate on the same basis, fostering a dynamic exchange between consumers and businesses in the digital marketplace.

The C2B (Consumer-to-Business) e-commerce model is characterized by several general features that define its dynamics and interactions between consumers and businesses:

- **Direct Action:** C2B involves direct action where individual consumers take the initiative to approach businesses actively. Consumers independently engage with businesses, offering products, services, feedback, or ideas.

- **Collaborative Consumption:** Collaborative consumption is a key feature, emphasizing the shared use of goods and services. Consumers collaborate with businesses in various ways, such as providing reviews, sharing feedback, or contributing to the co-creation of products.

- **Detailed Segmentation:** C2B often involves detailed segmentation of consumer preferences and requirements. Businesses may tailor their offerings based on specific customer needs, leading to a more personalized and targeted approach.

- **Interaction:** Interaction is a fundamental aspect of C2B. Consumers actively engage with businesses through various online channels, such as websites, social media, and forums. This interaction facilitates communication, feedback, and the exchange of ideas.

- **Reciprocity:** Reciprocity is observed in C2B transactions, with consumers offering products, services, or insights to businesses in exchange for value. This reciprocal relationship can lead to mutual benefits for both parties involved.

- **Bi-Directionality:** C2B transactions are characterized by bi-directionality, meaning that communication and value exchange flow in both directions. Consumers provide input to businesses, and businesses respond by offering products and services or addressing consumer needs.

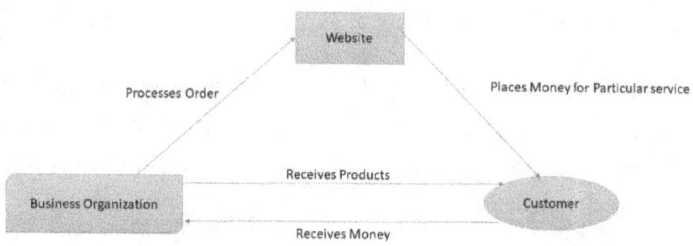

The emergence of the C2B (Consumer-to-Business) model can be attributed to significant changes driven by two key factors:

Bidirectional Network Connectivity: The ability to connect a large group of people through a bidirectional network facilitated by the internet has enabled the establishment of the C2B commercial relationship. Traditional media outlets typically operate in a one-directional manner, broadcasting information to the audience. In contrast, the bidirectional nature of the internet allows consumers to engage with businesses actively, providing feedback, offering products or services, and participating in collaborative processes.

Decreased Technology Cost: The reduced cost of technology has played a pivotal role in the C2B model. Technologies that were once exclusive to large companies have become more accessible to individuals. This includes advancements in digital printing, acquisition technology, high-performance computers, and powerful software.

The democratization of technology empowers individuals to leverage sophisticated tools and platforms, enabling them to contribute to the business-consumer dynamic actively.

The C2B (Consumer-to-Business) model is only sometimes applicable to some companies, but certain entities have successfully embraced this trading approach. Examples of C2B schemes include online advertising sites like Google AdSense, affiliation platforms like Commission Junction, and affiliation programs like Amazon. In these models, individuals play an active role by displaying advertising banners or promoting products on their websites.

This direct engagement allows individuals to provide advertising and selling services to businesses.

This new C2B business model represents a revolutionary shift, introducing a collaborative trading scheme that paves the way for new applications and socio-economic behaviors. It empowers individuals to contribute to the business-consumer relationship actively, reshaping traditional commerce dynamics and fostering a more participatory approach in the digital landscape.

Advantages of the C2B (Consumer-to-Business)

- **Versatility in Description:** The C2B model can be effectively described using terms such as paths, nodes, and properties. This versatility allows for a comprehensive understanding of the model's structure and components.

- **Graphical Representation:** The C2B model can be visually represented through graphics. Examples and visualizations can be generated to illustrate the interactions and relationships within the model, enhancing clarity and comprehension.

- **Centralized Configuration:** All Magnolia configurable elements can be centralized in one place within the C2B model. This centralized configuration simplifies management and ensures a cohesive structure for various elements involved in consumer-to-business interactions.

- **Integration with Java Documentation:** The C2B model can still be linked to Java documentation, providing a seamless integration between the model and relevant documentation. This linkage enhances understanding and facilitates efficient development and maintenance processes.

2.5. Business-to-Government (B2G)

Business-to-Government (B2G) e-commerce revolves around businesses selling goods or services to governments or government agencies.

This type of e-commerce involves supplying various entities, such as the military, police force, hospitals, and schools, with the necessary products and services.

Additionally, businesses engage in online competition for contracts to deliver services on behalf of the government, which may include tax collection and the provision of public services.

The exchange of information, services, and products between business organizations and government agencies takes place online. This interaction may encompass the following:

E-procurement services: Businesses learn about the purchasing needs of government agencies and provide the necessary services.

Virtual workplace: Businesses and government agencies collaborate online to coordinate work on contracted projects. This collaboration involves online meetings, plan reviews, and progress management.

Rental of online applications and databases: Specialized applications and databases designed for use by government agencies are rented by businesses to meet their specific needs.

2.6. Government-to-Business (G-to-B)

Government-to-Business, also known as e-government, involves the exchange of information, services, and products between government agencies and business organizations. Government websites now facilitate the exchange of:

Information, guidance, and advice for businesses: Pertaining to international trading, sources of funding and support (e.g., ukishelp), and facilities (e.g., www.dti.org.uk).

Database of laws, regulations, and government policy: Businesses can access information specific to their industry sectors.

Online application and submission of official forms: For processes such as value-added tax, businesses can submit forms electronically.

Online payment facilities: Businesses can make payments securely online.

2.7. Other Emerging Business Models

2.7.1. Business-to-Peer Networks (B-to-P)

In this model, businesses provide hardware, software, or other services to peer networks.

A notable example is Napster, which offered the software and infrastructure to facilitate peer networking.

2.7.2. Consumer-to-Government (C-to-G)

As of now, examples where consumers provide services to the government have yet to be widely implemented. Refer to the Government-to-Business model for related interactions.

2.7.3. Consumer-to-Peer Networks (C-to-P)

This concept is inherent in peer-to-peer networking, making the distinction slightly redundant.

In consumer-to-peer networks, consumers contribute their computing facilities once they become part of the peer network.

2.7.4. Government-to-Consumer (G-to-C)

Also known as e-government, this model involves government sites providing information, forms, and facilities for individuals to conduct transactions. Examples include paying bills and submitting official forms online, such as tax returns.

2.7.5. Government-to-Government (G-to-G)

Also referred to as e-government, this model encompasses transactions between governments within countries and on an international level.

This is particularly relevant within the European Union, where coordinated strategies are being developed to link different national systems.

2.7.6. Peer-to-Peer Network (P-to-P)

This communication model involves parties with the same capabilities, allowing either party to initiate a communication session. In recent usage, it refers to applications where users can directly exchange files over the Internet or through a mediating server.

2.7.7. Peer Network-to-Consumer (P-to-C)

This is peer-to-peer networking, offering services to consumers who are an integral part of the peer network.

2.7.8. Peer Network-to-Business (P-to-B)

Peer-to-peer networking provides resources to businesses. For instance, it utilizes peer network resources, such as the spare processing capacity of individual machines on the network, to solve complex problems like mathematical computations or intensive and repetitive DNA analyses that require high-capacity processing power.

2.7.9. Brokerage Model

The Brokerage Model in e-commerce mirrors its offline counterpart, where brokers act as intermediaries, bringing buyers and sellers together and facilitating transactions. In this model, brokers charge fees for their services. The unique advantage of e-commerce lies in its global reach, allowing brokers to connect buyers and sellers on a global scale, unlike the limitations faced by offline brokers restricted to local markets.

For instance, in the offline world, a mortgage broker linking potential homebuyers with financial institutions might be confined to their local region, limiting the pool of potential buyers. In contrast, an e-commerce mortgage broker, thanks to the internet's global nature, can reach individuals outside their immediate area, spanning states and countries.

This expanded reach significantly increases the number of potential buyers, enhancing the broker's ability to connect more buyers with sellers and, consequently, boost profits. eBay stands out as a prime example of a successful Auction Broker in e-commerce.

eBay, like many web-based companies, employs multiple business models to generate revenue. While the dominant model is the Brokerage model, eBay also leverages affiliate marketing, advertising, and community-driven models to maintain its presence and success in the e-commerce landscape.

Brokers play a pivotal role across various market segments, including business-to-business (B2B), business-to-consumer (B2C), and consumer-to-consumer (C2C) markets. Typically, brokers charge a fee or commission for the services they provide in facilitating transactions. The formula for these fees can vary based on the specific brokerage model being utilized. Some common brokerage models include:

Marketplace Exchange: Provides a comprehensive range of services throughout the transaction process for a specific industry. The exchange may operate independently or be supported by an industry consortium. Brokers typically charge sellers a transaction fee based on the sale's value, and there may be additional membership fees.

Business Trading Community: Also known as a vertical web community, it serves as a comprehensive hub for information and interaction within a specific vertical market. These communities may include product information, industry news, articles, job listings, and classifieds.

Buy/Sell Fulfilment: Customers specify buy or sell orders for a product or service, including details like price and delivery. The broker charges the buyer and seller a transaction fee.

Demand Collection System: Utilizes the "name-your-price" model pioneered by platforms like Priceline. Prospective buyers make final (binding) bids for specified goods or services, and the broker arranges fulfillment.

Auction Broker: Conducts auctions for sellers, charging a listing fee and commission based on the transaction value. Auctions may vary in terms of offering and bidding rules, with reverse auctions being a common variant.

Transaction Broker: Provides a third-party payment mechanism for buyers and sellers to settle transactions.

Bounty Broker: Offers a reward for finding specific items or information. The broker may list items for a flat fee and a percentage of the reward for items that are found.

Distributor: Operates as a catalog connecting product manufacturers with volume and retail buyers. Brokers facilitate transactions between franchised distributors and their trading partners.

Search Agent: Utilizes software agents or "robots" to search for the price and availability of a specified good or service or to locate hard-to-find information.

Virtual Mall: Hosts online merchants, charging setup, monthly listing, and per-transaction fees. More advanced malls may provide automated transaction services and opportunities for relationship marketing.

2.7.10. Value Chain Model

A product's value chain represents the sequence of activities performed by a business to enhance and deliver the product. These activities, undertaken by companies, encompass the entire process of creating and delivering products and services to customers. The value chain includes various stages, such as understanding customer needs, product design, material procurement, production, product storage, distribution, after-sales services, and customer care.

The primary purpose of value chain activities is to add value to the product at each stage before it reaches the customers. This value chain is composed of two main components: primary activities and secondary activities. Primary activities are directly linked to product manufacturing, including supply management and plant operations.

45

Secondary activities, on the other hand, are support functions like finance, human resources, and information technology.

G. Winfield Treese and Lawrence C. Stewart propose four broad value-chain areas:

Attract: Involves gaining and maintaining customer interest, encompassing advertising and marketing.

Interact: Focuses on turning interests into orders, covering sales, and cataloging activities.

Act: Encompasses order management, including order capture, payment processing, and fulfillment.

React: Involves servicing customers, incorporating technical support, customer service, and order tracking.

In the era of advanced information and communication technology, many businesses have embraced the Internet as a medium for their operations. Online commercial activities, such as buying, selling, and auctioning, are collectively known as e-commerce.

The e-commerce value chain includes activities like electronic fund transfer, internet marketing, distribution channels, and supply chain management.

2.7.11. Advertising Model

The advertising model in the online realm is an evolution of the traditional media broadcast model. In this model, a website takes on the role of a broadcaster, offering content and services such as email, chat, and forums interspersed with advertising messages presented as banner ads. The revenue for the broadcaster is often predominantly or solely derived from these banner ads. The broadcaster can either create content or act as a distributor of content produced elsewhere. The effectiveness of the advertising model hinges on the presence of a substantial or highly specialized volume of viewer traffic.

2.7.12. M-commerce

Mobile commerce, or m-commerce, refers to the buying and selling of goods and services through wireless technology, primarily on handheld devices such as cellular phones and personal digital assistants (PDAs). Japan is recognized as a global leader in e-commerce.

As content delivery over **wireless** devices becomes faster, more secure, and more scalable, some anticipate that m-commerce will surpass wireline e-commerce as the preferred method for digital commerce transactions.

Industries affected by m-commerce include:

Financial Services: This encompasses mobile banking and brokerage services, allowing users to manage their finances and investments on the go.

Telecommunications: Mobile devices serve as a central hub for various services, including making service changes, processing bill payments, and reviewing account details.

Service/Retail: Consumers can place and pay for orders using their mobile devices, providing on-the-fly convenience for various services and retail transactions.

Information Services: M-commerce facilitates the delivery of entertainment content, financial news, sports updates, and traffic information directly to mobile devices.

2.8. Summary

An electronic business model is a foundational framework for the development of e-commerce system applications, providing crucial design rationale from a business perspective. The precise definition and specification of an e-business model remain open questions, underscoring ongoing challenges in this field.

The Internet has introduced innovative business models to both Business-to-Business (B2B) and Business-to-Consumer (B2C) markets, reshaping the value chain and placing increasing pressure on all players, especially intermediaries, to add value or risk obsolescence.

The shortened value chain, influenced by the Internet, emphasizes the significance of efficiency and value addition, particularly for intermediaries. This evolving landscape of e-commerce requires continuous adaptation and innovation in business models to stay competitive and relevant in the market.

CHAPTER 3: SETTING UP AN E-COMMERCE BUSINESS

"In the vast landscape of E-Commerce, each transaction is a brushstroke, painting a tapestry of digital possibilities that weave together innovation and connectivity, creating a masterpiece of modern commerce."

Starting up an online store can be pretty thrilling. You're all hyped up about it, ready to dive into the digital world. But here's the deal – it's not just about getting a cool website up and running. Let me tell you a little story.

During the whole COVID-19 chaos, many regular stores thought, "Hey, let's go online to survive." They figured it was as easy as setting up a website, throwing in PayPal, and voila – open for business. But guess what? It's not that simple.

Launching an online business needs more thought than just having a flashy website. You've got to plan things out, think about which platforms will work best, and make sure everything runs like a well-oiled machine. And here's the kicker – once your shop is live, you can't just kick back and relax. You've got to figure out how to spread the word so people actually come and buy your stuff.

The COVID-19 rush made a bunch of companies jump into the online game, thinking it was a quick fix. But here's the reality – starting an online gig is more like cooking up a good meal. It would be best if you had the right ingredients and a solid recipe for success.

So, here's the takeaway: starting an online shop is about more than just putting it out there on the internet. It's about having a game plan right from the start and keeping the momentum going. It's a journey, from setting up shop to making sure folks know you're there and want to shop with you. So, buckle up; it's going to be an exciting ride!

3.1. Planning your eCommerce Business

Embarking on the journey of an e-commerce business requires meticulous planning and a deep understanding of various critical factors.

In this chapter, we'll explore considerations, potential pitfalls, and strategic goal-setting for a successful e-commerce venture.

3.1.1. Considerations: Building a Robust Foundation

As you lay the groundwork for your e-commerce website, the first crucial question emerges: Is your business geared towards exclusive online sales, and is your infrastructure aligned for a seamless transition?

- **Procurement Process: Securing Your Products**

  Delving into the procurement process is the first step in ensuring a robust foundation for your e-commerce business. Contemplate how you will acquire your products for the platform, whether through in-house manufacturing or strategic partnerships with suppliers. This decision forms the backbone of your inventory and influences your overall business strategy.

- **Storage Solutions: Safeguarding Your Inventory**

  Consider the logistics of product storage as a pivotal aspect of your operational model. Evaluate options ranging from traditional warehousing to contemporary drop shipping approaches. Choosing a storage solution that aligns seamlessly with your business scale and model is crucial for maintaining efficient operations and meeting customer demands.

- **Compelling Content: Persuading Purchase Decisions**

In the digital landscape, content plays a pivotal role in engaging and persuading potential customers. Identify the type of content that will captivate your audience and drive them to make a purchase.

This includes crafting compelling product descriptions, utilizing high-quality imagery, and potentially incorporating informative videos. A persuasive content strategy is integral to establishing a strong online presence.

- **Efficient Delivery: Fulfilling Customer Expectations**

Post-sales, the efficiency of your delivery system becomes paramount. Map out a robust strategy that considers logistics, collaborates with reliable shipping partners, and ensures customer expectations are not only met but exceeded. A seamless delivery process contributes significantly to customer satisfaction and loyalty.

- **Stock Management: Preparing for Success**

Anticipating the surge in business, implement an efficient stock management system. This proactive step ensures organized operations, minimizes the risk of stockouts, and enables you to adapt to varying demands. A well-managed inventory is fundamental to sustaining business growth.

- **Brand Integration: Harmonizing Tradition and Innovation**

Whether you're a new entrant or transitioning from a brick-and-mortar business, leverage existing brand credibility and customer bases from physical stores. The integration of your brand across both online and offline channels creates a unified and recognizable identity.

- **Physical Store Synergy: Bridging the Gap**

Explore synergies between your physical store and the e-commerce platform. Services like click-and-collect or synchronized promotions contribute to a cohesive brand image and enhance the overall customer experience. The collaboration between physical and online stores provides customers with diverse yet interconnected avenues to interact with your brand.

- **Holistic Customer Experience: Merging Digital and Tangible**

C22 considers the coexistence of physical and online stores as an opportunity to offer customers a holistic and targeted experience aligned with their buying habits. The integration of digital and tangible elements contributes to a seamless and enriching customer journey, fostering brand loyalty and satisfaction.

3.1.2. Pitfalls: Navigating Challenges

- **Resource Alignment: Tailoring Your E-commerce Fit**

Check how well your existing resources match your e-commerce plans. Going online needs a good look at what you've got right now. Some businesses might need help to shift to selling online because of their current setup. This involves checking if your team has the right skills, if your tech is up to speed, and if you can handle the practical side of things. Doing this makes sure your move to online sales is not just smooth but also a smart fit for success.

- **Business Model Comprehension: Avoiding Missteps**

The way e-commerce works is different from your usual business setup. There are unique models like selling to other businesses (B2B), selling to consumers (B2C), or drop shipping. Suppose you need to get how this works; you might end up with a strategy that doesn't match what your customers want. So, it's important to know these models well to pick the one that suits your business.

- **Capital Investment Insight: Grasping True Costs**

Starting and keeping up an online store comes with various costs. From getting your website ready, creating content, dealing with payment systems, shipping things out, and getting legal help – all these need money.

If you don't figure out the true costs from the start, you might end up short on funds. Understanding what you really need to spend helps you plan better and avoid money troubles.

3.1.3. Setting Objectives: Crafting Your Path

- **Manufacturing: Emotional Investment and Risk Dynamics**

When you make things yourself, it's not just a business move; it's personal. You put your heart into what you create. But here's the catch – having a bunch of products comes with risks, especially if they are hard to sell.

If things don't go as planned, you might end up with a lot of unsold stock, which can be a tough challenge.

- **Drop Shipping: Less Risk, More Reliance**

In drop shipping, you don't own the products. That's a relief because you don't have to worry about stock sitting on shelves.

But it comes with its own set of challenges. You depend on suppliers to have what your customers want, and you're at the mercy of their prices.

If they decide to charge more, your profits could take a hit.

3.1.4. Uncovering Opportunities: Strategic Insights

- **Competitor Analysis: A Google Expedition**

Use Google as your ultimate tool for research. Identify and analyze your industry competitors. Look at what they're doing - their strategies, what products they offer, how they price things, and how they connect with their audience. This detective work helps you figure out your unique approach. Knowing your competition inside out is like having a map for your journey; it guides you on where to go and how to stand out.

- **Industry Trends: Staying Ahead**

Stay in the loop with what's hot in your industry. Trends can make or break your business. Keep yourself updated on what's happening in your market. Understand the trends, and you'll be in a better position to offer something better than your competitors. It's like surfing the wave rather than getting washed away by it. Being ahead of the curve gives you a competitive edge.

- **Social Listening and Alerts: Real-Time Market Vigilance**

Social media is where your customers chat. Listen to their conversations to understand what they like or dislike about your brand and your competitors. Setting up alerts, like Google Alerts, is like having a radar for emerging trends. You don't want to miss out on what's happening in real time. This kind of vigilance keeps you on your toes and ensures you're always in tune with the market.

3.2. Setting Up Your E-commerce Store

As you embark on the journey of establishing your e-commerce store, it's crucial to understand the key elements that constitute a successful online presence. Let's break down these elements and explore some popular e-commerce platforms:

3.2.1. Website Elements

Home Page: Your online 'storefront,' the home page is where you showcase your brand and entice visitors to explore further.

Category Pages: Organized category pages facilitate easy navigation, enhancing the customer experience and encouraging cross-selling and impulse purchases.

Product Pages: The focal point for driving conversions, product pages should provide comprehensive information and persuasive elements.

Shopping Cart: Enables customers to initiate the conversion process, offering insights into their experiences. Pay attention to reducing cart abandonment rates.

Checkout: Customer experience is paramount here. Ensure a clear and simple purchase process to minimize the risk of customers leaving the website.

Navigation, Site Search, and Filters: General elements like navigation, site search, and filters contribute to simplifying the customer journey. Consider principles of digital accessibility for diverse customer needs.

3.2.2. Main E-commerce Platforms

➤ **Shopify:**

It stands out as an excellent choice for rapidly establishing and optimizing e-commerce ventures, especially tailored for small to medium-sized businesses. Renowned for its user-friendly interface and reliable technology, Shopify accommodates entrepreneurs seeking efficient solutions for their online presence in the dynamic realm of digital commerce.

Setup: Quick and easy setup, starting at $29 a month.

Technology: Secure and reliable platform, suitable for small to medium-sized organizations.

Support: Robust community support and customer support are available.

Customizable: Offers pre-built sites using optimized themes or customization for specific needs.

SEO: Good SEO features and marketing integrations.

Abandoned Checkout Recovery: Built-in feature for recovering abandoned checkouts via email.

Payment Gateways: It integrates with various gateways, including PayPal and Stripe.

Consideration: Prices can escalate with larger enterprise-level offerings.

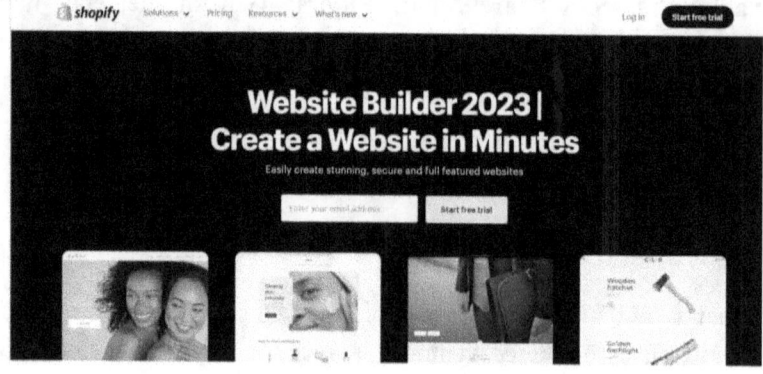

➤ **WooCommerce:**

In the realm of e-commerce, WooCommerce emerges as a compelling choice, and its most alluring feature is its essentially free nature. Here's a snapshot of the key characteristics that define the WooCommerce experience:

Open-Source Brilliance:

As an integral part of the WordPress ecosystem, WooCommerce operates on an open-source model, making it not only cost-effective but also highly customizable. Integrating WooCommerce into your WordPress site is as simple as adding a widget, empowering you to manage your e-commerce endeavors effortlessly.

Limitless Customization:

WooCommerce inherits the famed customizable features synonymous with WordPress. This means you have the creative freedom to tailor your online store to align with your brand's unique identity and customer preferences.

User-Friendly Dynamics:

For those well-acquainted with the user-friendly environment of WordPress, setting up a WooCommerce website becomes a seamless process.

The familiarity ensures a smooth onboarding experience, allowing you to focus more on your products and less on technical intricacies.

Mobile Optimization Mastery:

Recognizing the prominence of mobile commerce, WooCommerce ensures that your online store is optimized for mobile devices. This commitment to mobile responsiveness caters to a tech-savvy audience that prefers the convenience of on-the-go shopping.

SEO Empowerment:

WooCommerce provides the tools to optimize your online store for search engines. This SEO-friendly approach enhances your visibility, ensuring that potential customers can easily discover your products in the vast digital landscape.

Community-Backed Support:

With WooCommerce being an integral part of the WordPress family, you gain access to a robust community support system. This collaborative environment allows you to seek assistance, share insights, and navigate any challenges that may arise during your e-commerce journey.

Content Marketing Prowess:

Harnessing the content marketing prowess of WordPress, WooCommerce becomes an ideal platform for content-driven marketing strategies. Leveraging blogs and content marketing initiatives becomes a seamless endeavor, amplifying your brand's online presence.

Gateway Integration Excellence:

Similar to Shopify, WooCommerce seamlessly integrates with a multitude of payment gateways, providing flexibility and convenience for both merchants and customers. This broad spectrum of integrated gateways ensures a smooth and secure transaction experience.

WooCommerce is the
platform that grows
with you

No matter what success looks like for you, you can do it with WooCommerce. Our WordPress-based ecommerce platform helps merchants and developers build successful businesses for the long term

Try it free for 14 days, then upgrade to any paid plan for only $1 for your first 3 months.*

➤ **Wix:**

For those venturing into the realm of global e-commerce, a Wix e-commerce site stands out as an accessible starting point, particularly tailored for beginners. Let's unravel the key characteristics that define the Wix experience:

User-Friendly Launchpad:

Wix positions itself as an ideal choice for beginners in the e-commerce landscape. Its user-friendly interface makes the setup process relatively straightforward, catering to small businesses taking their initial steps into the digital marketplace. Although it offers limited stock tracking functionality, this simplicity aligns with the needs of those commencing their online ventures.

Affordability at Its Core:

Affordability becomes a hallmark of Wix, with pricing ranging between $17 and $25 per month. This cost-effective model makes it an attractive option for budget-conscious entrepreneurs seeking a digital storefront without breaking the bank.

Intuitive Design Dynamics:

Building a website on Wix is notably easier compared to some other platforms. Its intuitive drag-and-drop interface allows users to effortlessly rearrange elements, providing a seamless experience in crafting a visually appealing and functional online space.

Versatile Widgets for Enhancement:

Wix enhances its functionality through the incorporation of diverse widgets and features.

This versatility allows users to extend the capabilities of their website, customizing it to meet specific business requirements and user expectations.

Aesthetic Diversity with Templates:

Dive into a pool of design diversity with Wix's array of templates. Whether you seek a sleek and modern look or a more traditional aesthetic, Wix provides a multitude of designs to choose from, allowing you to tailor your online presence to align with your brand identity.

Gateway Integration Harmony:

Just like its counterparts, Shopify and WooCommerce, Wix seamlessly integrates with various payment gateways. This ensures a smooth and secure transaction process for both merchants and customers, contributing to a hassle-free online shopping experience.

> **BigCommerce:**

Entrepreneurs with growing ventures may find BigCommerce appealing. Renowned for its scalability, it caters to businesses of varying sizes. With a focus on user-friendliness, it offers features like responsive templates, a robust inventory system, and built-in SEO tools.

> **OpenCart: Open-Source Flexibility:**

OpenCart, an open-source platform, provides flexibility and adaptability. It suits businesses seeking customization options without the need for extensive technical expertise. With a straightforward setup and a range of extensions, it caters to diverse e-commerce needs.

These examples, including Squarespace and Magento, showcase the array of choices available. The key lies in aligning the features and strengths of each platform with the unique requirements of your business, ensuring a seamless and successful venture into the digital marketplace.

3.3. Building an online store

In the world of small businesses, reaching new customers is key to growth, and the Internet offers a great opportunity for this. It not only allows you to expand your sales to a broader audience but also levels the playing field against bigger competitors. If worries about costs and technology have been holding you back from selling online, here's some good news—starting a website is more affordable than you might think. With user-friendly technology and available experts, getting online to boost your sales is within reach.

Isn't it time you took your business online?

Is Your Product a Good Fit for E-Commerce?

The success stories of numerous small businesses attaining remarkable profits online underscore the potential that the digital sphere holds. However, the suitability of selling products on the Internet hinges on your specific business and product line. To gauge this, consider the following guidelines:

Product Comprehension: Is your product easy for online customers to understand? Given that shoppers can't physically interact with the product, comprehensive product descriptions, high-quality photographs, clear return policies, and positive reviews become crucial in alleviating buyer apprehension.

Profitability: Can you sell your product at a profit once you factor in packaging and delivery costs? If you're selling low-cost items, you might need to sell in larger quantities to make a profit. For perishable items, quick delivery and proper packaging are essential.

Digital Delivery: If you provide services or digital products, can they be efficiently delivered online or via email? Many service providers have successfully transitioned to the Internet, such as converting magazines to digital editions.

Geographic Appeal: Does your product cater to customers beyond your local area, or will online sales enhance service to existing customers? Consider the potential reach of your product and whether it aligns with online selling.

3.4. Building Your Online Presence

3.4.1. Register Your Domain

The first step in establishing your online business is securing a domain name or URL. This unique address is crucial for your digital identity. Be creative if your first choice is taken, but avoid confusion with similar names. Domain names consist of your unique name and a top-level domain (TLD), like .com or .net. Protect exclusivity by considering registration for multiple TLDs. Various domain registrars, such as 1&1, ENOM, GoDaddy, and Network Solutions, offer registration for prices ranging from $10 to $30 per year.

3.4.2. Build Your Site

Do It Yourself:

In the journey of setting up your e-commerce business, the pivotal step is building your online store. This process demands thoughtful consideration of elements and the selection of a platform aligned with your unique requirements.

As we've discussed previously, platforms like Wix, Shopify, and WooCommerce offer distinct advantages.

Hire a Web Designer/Developer:

Rely on a web developer for a professionally crafted online store. Choose an Authorize.Net Certified Developer for expertise and convenience. The Certified Developer Directory on Authorize.Net can assist in finding a suitable professional.

Host Your Site

A web hosting company provides server space, internet connectivity, email management, and other services to make your website accessible online.

Choose a reliable hosting service to ensure seamless operations for your business.

3.4.3. Facilitating Secure Online Payments

With your online store ready, the next crucial step is to empower customers with the ability to make seamless online purchases. This involves setting up a robust payment gateway and ensuring the security of online transactions.

Merchant Account: The Foundation of Transactions

A merchant account from a financial institution is essential for collecting payments from consumer bank or credit card accounts. While a Card Present (CP) merchant account may suffice for retail sales, a Card Not Present (CNP) merchant account is necessary for online transactions. ISOs, MSPs, and VARs are key entities offering merchant accounts. The Authorize.Net Reseller Directory or your current banking partner can guide you in obtaining a CNP merchant account.

Payment Gateway Account: Enabling Secure Transactions

Payment gateways, exemplified by Authorize.Net, provide the infrastructure for merchants to accept credit card and electronic check payments online. This virtual substitute for physical card swipe machines securely processes payment data, communicates with financial institutions, and facilitates the transfer of proceeds into the merchant account.

Credit Card Payment Flow: A Seamless Transaction Journey

Understanding the intricacies of the credit card payment process is crucial for a smooth and secure transaction experience.

Authorization Phase: Ensuring Validity and Availability

The process commences with the customer initiating a payment.

Authorize.Net takes charge and routes payment details to credit card networks on behalf of the merchant.

The credit card networks validate the payment information and check fund availability.

Based on the validation, the network returns results—either approving or declining the transaction.

The merchant is promptly informed of the authorization status.

Settlement/Funding Phase: Transfer of Transaction Funds

After authorization, the customer's credit card issuing bank initiates the transfer of appropriate funds for the transaction.

The funds are sent to the merchant's bank, and within two to four business days, the bank deposits the funds into the merchant's account.

3.4.4. Promote Your Business: Elevating Visibility and Attracting Customers

After establishing your online store, it's pivotal to deploy effective and budget-friendly strategies to promote your business and captivate customers.

Search Engine Optimization (SEO): Enhancing Online Visibility

Traditional SEO involves refining your website's content and structure to align with relevant keywords, improving its search engine ranking. This cost-free method optimizes text and page layout for better search results. Post-optimization, submit your site for inclusion in search engine results.

Link Building is a more intricate SEO approach aiming to boost search engine ranking by increasing links to your website across the Internet. Search engines perceive these links as "votes" for your site's importance. Establishing relevant, quality inbound links is crucial. Link-building methods can be either free or paid, depending on the source providing the link.

Pay Per Click Advertising: Boost Visibility with Strategic Online Ads

Engaging in pay-per-click (PPC) advertising is a dynamic strategy to enhance your online presence by having your ad displayed when specific keywords or phrases are searched on Internet search engines. In this model, you pay for the service each time a user clicks on your ad.

The cost of a PPC ad is influenced by the competitiveness of your chosen keywords and the significance of the search engine platform. These ads typically appear labeled as "Sponsored Links," distinguishing them from organic search results. To streamline your PPC efforts, Authorize.Net collaborates with various Pay-Per-Click (PPC) providers to boost your website's visibility. For a comprehensive array of third-party solutions aiding your business operations and marketing endeavors, explore the Authorize.Net Merchant Toolbox.

Web.com: Empower Your Online Presence

Recognizing the significance of your website investment, Web.com introduces a holistic small business Internet marketing program tailored to propel you ahead of the competition. Their innovative service, Visibility Online, blends search engine and Internet directory listings to streamline promotional efforts. Explore more at Web.com.

Email Marketing with MailChimp: Streamline Communication

Simplify customer communication and foster repeat business with MailChimp, an award-winning service trusted by thousands worldwide. Seamlessly send HTML email newsletters, holiday promotions, and special announcements to your customers. Learn more at MailChimp.

Social Media Engagement: Direct Connections

Connect directly with customers on social media platforms like Twitter, Facebook, and LinkedIn. These channels facilitate product announcements, promotions, and customer interactions without the need for an extensive web development team.

"Offline" Marketing Strategies: Integrate Your Web Presence

Incorporate your website address into all printed materials, including advertisements, business cards, stationery, and Yellow Pages ads.

Announce your online store's launch to customers via email if you have their addresses, ensuring they are aware of the new shopping avenue.

3.4.5. Secure Your Transactions with Authorize. Net's Security Services

Ensure the safety of your transactions with Authorize.Net's advanced security offerings:

Advanced Fraud Detection Suite™ (AFDS): Identify, Manage, Prevent Fraud

Authorize.Net's AFDS empowers you to recognize, handle, and prevent suspicious and potentially costly fraudulent transactions. Utilize customizable, rules-based filters and tools to enhance security.

Comodo SSL Certificates: Establish Secure Connections

For a secure connection between your website and the Authorize.Net Payment Gateway, leverage Comodo SSL certificates. As a leading provider, Comodo extends a significant discount to Authorize.Net merchants.

FreshBooks Integration: Streamline Business Management

Integrate FreshBooks, a swift invoicing and time-tracking service, with your Authorize.Net account.

Manage your business efficiently by tracking time, invoicing clients, generating reports, and accepting payments seamlessly.

3.5. Logistics and Fulfillment

In the realm of e-commerce, the journey doesn't conclude with a successful online transaction. The logistics and fulfillment processes are the unsung heroes that ensure the seamless transition from a customer clicking "Buy Now" to the actual delivery of the purchased product. Let's explore these crucial aspects in detail.

Order Processing Workflow:

Once a customer completes a purchase, the journey kicks off with the order confirmation. This isn't just a transactional email; it's a digital handshake, assuring the customer that their order is received, correct, and acknowledged. This initial communication sets the tone for what follows.

Inventory management steps into the spotlight at this juncture. Regular vigilance over stock levels is paramount. In a world of instant gratification, the last thing you want is a disappointed customer discovering that their eagerly awaited item is out of stock. Investing in a robust inventory management system ensures real-time tracking and prevents overselling.

The next act in this orchestration is the packing and shipping process. Packaging isn't just about putting items in a box; it's about safeguarding a customer's anticipation.

Quality materials and meticulous methods ensure that the product arrives not just intact but in a presentation that mirrors the care you put into your business.

But the story doesn't end there. A modern consumer expects to be in the know. Order tracking becomes your protagonist, offering customers a virtual window into the journey of their purchase. This transparency reduces anxiety, fosters trust, and provides a sense of participation in the entire process.

The climax is the delivery confirmation. This is the point where the digital journey transforms into a tangible experience. A confirmation upon delivery acts as the curtain call, assuring the customer that their package has safely arrived and completing the transaction loop.

Optimizing Logistics:

Selecting the appropriate shipping partners is comparable to assembling a skilled ensemble for a theatrical performance. Reliability, cost-effectiveness, and delivery speed are the criteria for this casting call. Negotiating partnerships with carriers that align with your business ethos ensures that the last mile of the journey is as impressive as the first.

Packaging solutions contribute not only to protection but also to your brand's sustainability narrative, in an era where environmental consciousness is a significant player in consumer choices, eco-friendly packaging positions your business as one that cares.

For those with global aspirations, international shipping is a chapter that requires careful consideration. Simplifying processes, understanding customs regulations, and transparently communicating international shipping costs can turn this logistical challenge into a strategic advantage.

Returns and exchanges, often seen as the conclusion in e-commerce, don't have to be an unwelcome ending. Clearly, explaining return policies and simplifying the process can transform a potentially negative experience into a chance to highlight excellent customer service.

Continuous Improvement:

In the world of logistics and fulfillment, the final curtain doesn't mark the end; it signals the beginning of improvement. Customer feedback becomes your script for the next act. Encouraging customers to share their experiences through surveys or reviews provides invaluable insights into areas of excellence and areas for refinement. Performance analytics serve as your exclusive backstage pass, offering a sneak peek behind the scenes. Examining logistics performance, pinpointing bottlenecks, monitoring delivery times, and assessing the effectiveness of shipping partners are all crucial elements of the ongoing improvement storyline.

In the grand production of e-commerce, logistics and fulfillment are the backstage crew, ensuring that every scene plays out seamlessly, leaving the audience (your customers) with a standing ovation.

3.6. Summary

Embarking on the e-commerce journey involves careful planning and strategic decision-making. From establishing a robust foundation and navigating challenges to setting objectives and uncovering opportunities, each step plays a vital role. Building an online store requires understanding its elements and choosing the right platform, while security is paramount in accepting online payments.

Promoting the business involves leveraging SEO, pay-per-click advertising, and various marketing services. Logistics and fulfillment are crucial, resembling casting the right actors in a play. Returns and exchanges, often viewed as outcomes, can be turned into positive experiences through user-friendly policies. Performance analytics act as a backstage pass, providing insights for continuous improvement. The essence lies in creating a seamless and thriving e-commerce venture, weaving together these elements into a cohesive narrative of success.

CHAPTER 4: E-MARKETING

"Create, communicate, and deliver value to a target market at a profit."

– Philip Kotler

4.1. Introduction

In today's digital world, businesses are increasingly embracing e-marketing, also known as electronic marketing, as a crucial part of their strategies. You might hear it called Online Marketing or Internet Marketing, too. Why? Because it's a valuable tool for boosting online visibility and connecting with your audience. E-marketing, a pivotal trend in business marketing and information technology, stands as a transformative force. This approach has fundamentally altered how businesses promote their products and how interactions between businesses and consumers unfold. E-marketing encompasses diverse facets such as information management, public relations, customer services, and sales, earning it the moniker "internet marketing." Notably, it constitutes a crucial element within the broader realm of electronic commerce.

4.2. Meaning and Definition of E-Marketing

E-Marketing, also known as Internet Marketing or Online Marketing, is a way of promoting products or services using the Internet. It involves reaching the target audience through smartphones, devices, and social media. E-Marketing includes not only online methods but also email and wireless media. Businesses use various technologies to connect with their customers. It's a crucial part of integrated marketing communications (IMC), helping brands grow across different channels. Many companies incorporate e-marketing into their overall marketing strategy through various digital media channels.

E-marketing is the process of conducting marketing activities and achieving marketing objectives through electronic mediums. In simple terms, it involves using computer systems, the internet, and other electronic networks for the exchange of goods or services, where their values in terms of price are determined.

According to CISCO specialists, e-marketing encompasses all activities that businesses conduct through the Internet with the aim of attracting, winning, and retaining customers.

This involves utilizing online networks, computer communication, and digital interactive media to achieve the marketing goals of an organization. E-marketing enhances the functions of traditional marketing by incorporating strategies like email campaigns, banner ads, referrals, and video ads to attract and retain customers.

Instant platforms like Naukri.com facilitate job seekers in finding suitable placements at an economical cost. E-marketing means leveraging digital technology to sell goods and services, complementing traditional marketing methods. While businesses continue to use traditional marketing approaches such as advertising, direct, and PR, e-marketing adds a new dimension to the marketing mix. Its adaptability and cost-effectiveness render it suitable not just for large enterprises but also for small firms, with many businesses achieving impressive outcomes through e-marketing.

4.3. Importance and Benefits of E-Marketing

4.3.1. Importance of E-marketing

Importance in the realm of promoting sales consistently, unbound by specific dates or times. The flexibility to advertise products at any given moment widens the reach to a diverse customer base, fostering enduring customer relationships.

One key advantage is the ability to transcend geographical limitations, connecting with customers in remote areas without

72

constraints of distance. Unlike traditional marketing confined to specific locales, e-marketing permeates numerous remote regions, expanding market access.

Cost-effectiveness is a hallmark of e-marketing, circumventing the substantial expenses associated with establishing physical stores. The financial burden of rent, storage, and miscellaneous expenses is notably diminished, making it an attractive option for investors.

E-marketing excels in providing detailed product explanations and specifications, compellingly presenting them to potential buyers. Understanding consumer behavior and market trends through competitor analysis and target market studies facilitates the creation of tailored product profiles, catering to diverse customer segments and enhancing purchase likelihood.

Continuous communication between the company and customers post-purchase fosters a special bond, signaling consumer engagement. This ongoing interaction, facilitated through marketing new products, exclusive offers, and discounts via promotional emails, establishes a connection that encourages repeat purchases and loyalty.

In essence, e-marketing is not merely a promotional tool; it is a strategic approach that combines cost-effectiveness, comprehensive product presentation, market understanding, and continuous customer engagement to build enduring relationships and drive sustained business success.

4.3.2. Benefits of e-marketing

E-marketing stands as a pivotal asset for both business owners and consumers alike, offering a myriad of advantages. For consumers, one of the primary benefits lies in the accessibility of comprehensive product information. This is facilitated through avenues such as perusing friend reviews, conducting thorough searches, examining product reviews, and empowering buyers to make informed decisions.

Furthermore, e-marketing streamlines the purchasing process by providing convenient payment options, including the use of bank cards and various electronic payment methods, such as

Master Card and Visa. The seamless integration of these payment mechanisms contributes to a hassle-free and efficient transaction experience.

The expansive reach of the Internet is a key driver behind the surge in marketing clients and transactions facilitated by e-marketing. This widespread connectivity enables businesses to tap into a global customer base, resulting in a significant increase in both clientele and overall transactions.

Additionally, e-marketing transcends geographical constraints, allowing consumers to access and purchase products that may not be readily available in their local vicinity. The online marketplace becomes a gateway to a diverse array of products, offering consumers a broader selection than traditional retail avenues.

The scalability of e-marketing is another noteworthy advantage, as it eliminates the spatial constraints associated with traditional marketing. Unlike brick-and-mortar establishments that require substantial physical space for product displays, e-marketing operates in a virtual realm, saving businesses from expenses such as rent, taxes, and electricity. This cost efficiency translates to more competitive pricing for consumer, making products more affordable compared to their traditional market counterpart.

In essence, e-marketing revolutionizes the consumer experience by empowering individuals with information, convenience, global accessibility, product variety, and cost-saving, thereby redefining the landscape of modern commerce.

4.4. Marketing Challenge

1. Staying on Top of Trends

➢ Why it's challenging:

The fast-paced dynamics of digital platforms, epitomized by platforms like TikTok, underscore the difficulty of staying ahead of trends. The ever-evolving landscape, characterized by rapid shifts in user preferences and emerging trends, necessitates constant vigilance. For businesses, this translates into a significant, time-consuming commitment to monitor, analyze, and adapt to the ever-changing online environment.

➢ How to solve:

To surmount this challenge, businesses must adopt a strategic approach. Rather than attempting to chase every viral dance or meme, it is imperative to focus on trends that align with the specific industry. This targeted strategy ensures resource efficiency and maintains alignment with the brand's identity. By understanding and embracing industry-specific trends, businesses can navigate the evolving digital landscape more effectively, enhancing their online presence and resonance with the target audience.

2. Facing Competition

➢ Why it's challenging:

The relentless challenge of facing competition is exacerbated by the escalating number of businesses delving into digital marketing. The surge in competition constructs a scenario where distinguishing oneself becomes progressively arduous. In this saturated environment, the audience is bombarded with a myriad of alternatives, making it challenging for a business to carve its niche.

➤ **How to solve:**

Addressing this challenge necessitates a comprehensive competitor analysis. Understanding the strengths and weaknesses of competitors is pivotal.

This insight serves as a foundational element, empowering businesses to craft a robust digital marketing strategy. Tailoring strategies to the unique strengths and attributes of the business is essential for not only attracting but also retaining qualified leads in the fiercely competitive landscape.

3. Setting the Appropriate Budget

➤ **Why it's challenging:**

The formidable challenge of setting an appropriate budget looms large in marketing endeavors. Striking a balance between investing enough for effective marketing and avoiding unnecessary expenditure poses a perpetual dilemma.

The complexity deepens, particularly with strategies like PPC and social media ads, which need more definitive budgetary constraints.

➤ **How to solve:**

A prudent starting point is allocating 7-8% of the revenue to marketing, offering a foundational budgetary framework. However, this figure serves as a guide, and fine-tuning based on specific business requirements is essential.

Contextualizing the budget with industry benchmarks, such as the finding that 68% of businesses allocate $500-$10,000 per month for marketing, provides valuable additional insights.

4. Managing Data

➤ **Why it's challenging:**

The deluge of data stemming from digital marketing campaigns, encompassing clicks, leads, and conversions, presents a formidable challenge. The complexity lies in efficiently managing this wealth of data, involving intricate processes of collection, processing, and prioritization.

➤ **How to solve:**

Strategic investment in data management software, exemplified by tools like Marketing CloudFX, emerges as a pivotal solution. These platforms streamline the tracking and analysis of marketing campaigns, simplifying the otherwise arduous task. Clear articulation of campaign goals and a focused approach to pertinent data, encompassing metrics like click-through rates and form completions, ensures the team's concerted efforts align with overarching objectives.

5. Generating Quality Leads

➤ **Why it's challenging:**

The challenge of generating quality leads hinges on the nuanced tasks of precise targeting and fostering genuine interest. Pinpointing the right audience and tailoring marketing efforts to engage them authentically can prove intricate, demanding continuous refinement.

➤ **How to solve:**

Foundational to overcoming this challenge is the creation of detailed buyer personas crafted from real customer profiles. These personas, enriched with demographic details, buying habits, and other pertinent information, serve as a guiding compass for marketing strategies, ensuring resonance with the intended audience.

6. Finding the Right Marketing Tools

➤ **Why it's challenging:**

Identifying suitable marketing tools poses a challenge due to the abundance of options available. From email management to customer data processing, the multitude of tools requires careful consideration, especially when unsure of specific needs.

➤ **How to solve:**

To address this common marketing issue, leverage third-party resources like G2.com, offering unbiased analyses of different software types. Additionally, seek recommendations from your professional network to identify platforms that have received positive feedback. This ensures a more informed decision in selecting tools tailored to your requirements.

7. Adaptability

➤ **Why it's challenging:**

Adaptability in marketing is challenging as businesses tend to cling to familiar strategies that have previously worked. The reluctance to embrace change might lead to missed growth opportunities as marketing landscapes and technologies evolve.

➤ **How to solve:**

Foster an adaptable mindset by allocating a portion of the marketing budget to explore new channels. Continuously review existing marketing channels and reallocate budgets based on performance. This ensures a balance between proven strategies and the exploration of new opportunities for sustained growth.

8. Influencer Collaboration

➤ **Why it's challenging:**

Identifying and collaborating with the right influencers can be challenging, as it requires aligning the influencer's audience with the brand and ensuring authenticity in the partnership.

➤ **How to solve:**

Conduct thorough research to find influencers whose values and audience match your brand. Establish clear expectations and guidelines for collaboration to maintain authenticity. Utilize influencer marketing platforms or agencies to streamline the identification and collaboration process.

9. Measuring ROI (Return on Investment)

➤ **Why it's challenging:**

Measuring the effectiveness of marketing efforts and calculating the return on investment can be complex, especially with multiple channels and varied metrics.

➤ **How to solve:**

Implement tracking tools and analytics platforms to monitor key performance indicators (KPIs) across different channels. Set specific goals and tie them to measurable outcomes. Regularly evaluate and adjust your strategies based on the data to optimize ROI.

10. Creating Quality Content

➤ **Why it's challenging:**

Quality content creation is time-consuming as it requires thorough research, accurate information, and engaging presentation. This challenge is exacerbated for businesses with limited time and multiple projects.

➤ **How to solve:**

To address this challenge, businesses can create a content calendar to manage time effectively. Breaking down the content creation process into steps, such as research, writing, editing, and publishing on different days, can streamline the workflow. Alternatively, outsourcing content creation to a specialized agency can relieve businesses of this task.

11. Identifying and Entering New Markets

➤ **Why it's challenging:**

Identifying and entering new markets is challenging due to the complexities of market analysis and the need to determine the viability of each potential market. The established competition further complicates market entry strategies.

➤ **How to solve:**

To tackle this challenge, businesses can study their competitors and learn from their market expansion strategies. Analyzing competitors that have successfully tapped into new markets can provide valuable insights. Implementing proven marketing strategies and monitoring their effectiveness in the new market helps in refining and optimizing the approach.

12. Testing New Channels

➤ **Why it's challenging:**

Testing new marketing channels poses challenges due to the learning curve associated with unfamiliar platforms. Understanding the intricacies of new channels, especially those not previously utilized, can be overwhelming.

➢ **How to solve:**

The key solution lies in thorough research before venturing into new channels. Businesses can leverage industry expertise, learn about tools and strategies employed in these channels, and understand how to measure results effectively. Seeking guidance from industry experts or hiring a marketing company with experience in diverse channels can provide valuable support in navigating the challenges of testing new avenues.

13. Crisis Management

Why it's challenging:

Handling unexpected crises, such as negative public reactions or technical issues, can be challenging and requires a swift and effective response.

How to solve:

Develop a crisis management plan that outlines potential scenarios and appropriate responses. Monitor social media and other channels for early signs of issues. Act transparently and promptly address concerns to mitigate the impact of crises.

14. Globalization Challenges

Why it's challenging:

Expanding marketing efforts globally introduces challenges related to cultural differences, language barriers, and varying consumer behaviors.

How to solve:

Conduct thorough market research for each target region. Tailor marketing strategies to align with local cultures and preferences.

Utilize translation services and collaborate with local experts to ensure effective communication.

15. Employee Training and Engagement

Why it's challenging:

Ensuring that your team is well-trained and engaged in marketing initiatives can be challenging, especially with evolving technologies and strategies.

How to solve:

Invest in continuous training programs to keep your team updated on industry trends. Foster a collaborative and innovative work culture to enhance employee engagement. Encourage feedback and provide opportunities for professional development.

By addressing these challenges strategically, businesses can enhance their marketing effectiveness and navigate the ever-evolving digital landscape more successfully.

4.5. Summary

In the ever-evolving realm of digital commerce, this chapter delves into the profound domain of E-marketing, an indispensable facet of contemporary business strategies. Referred to interchangeably as electronic marketing, online marketing, or internet marketing, it stands as a transformative force shaping how businesses showcase products and engage with consumers. From information management to public relations and sales, E-marketing transcends traditional boundaries, earning the moniker "internet marketing" within the broader spectrum of electronic commerce.

This chapter unravels the meaning and essence of E-marketing, elucidating its role in promoting products and services through various digital channels, including smartphones, devices, and social media. A critical component of integrated marketing communications (IMC), E-marketing facilitates brand growth across diverse channels, harmonizing with both large enterprises and small firms.

Further, we discussed the importance and benefits of E-marketing, emphasizing its prowess in ensuring sales continuity, overcoming geographical constraints, and offering a cost-effective alternative to physical stores. It excels in providing detailed product information, fostering customer engagement, and building enduring relationships through continuous communication.

Additionally, the chapter outlines the challenges faced in the digital marketing landscape, ranging from staying abreast of trends to managing data and fostering employee engagement. Each challenge is met with strategic solutions, such as targeted trend focus, competitor analysis, budget allocation, and the adoption of data management tools.

In essence, this chapter is a comprehensive guide to navigating the intricacies of E-marketing, offering insights into its significance, benefits, and strategic approaches to surmount challenges, all narrated in the unique language of Booklish, where the digital and the traditional seamlessly converge.

CHAPTER 5: E-COMMERCE MARKETING STRATEGIES

"Strategies for business growth in e-commerce involve a dynamic blend of innovation, adaptability, and customer-centricity."

- Elon Musk

5.1. Introduction

A marketing strategy is a comprehensive plan designed to achieve specific marketing goals. It assesses the current strengths and gaps in your business related to the set objectives and devises tactics to meet those goals effectively.

This strategy outlines a company's overarching approach to reaching potential consumers and converting them into customers. It includes key elements such as the value proposition, brand messaging, and target customer demographics. It encompasses the four Ps of marketing: product, price, place, and promotion. In essence, it provides a focused and achievable roadmap for business success.

5.2 Understanding Marketing Strategies

A robust marketing strategy centers around the company's value proposition, conveying its identity, operational principles, and why it merits consumer patronage. This becomes a guiding template for marketing initiatives across all products and services.

For instance, Walmart is recognized as a discount retailer with a commitment to "everyday low prices," shaping its business operations and marketing endeavors. A well-crafted marketing strategy outlines specific goals, such as enhancing authority in niche circles, and the corresponding marketing plan translates these objectives into actionable steps, such as creating thought leadership pieces on platforms like LinkedIn.

Creating a Marketing Strategy

- **Identify Goals:** Define overarching goals and short-term objectives such as authority establishment, increased engagement, or lead generation.

- **Know Your Clients:** Understand your ideal customer, their preferences, and the platforms they frequent.

- **Create Your Message**: Craft compelling messages that showcase how your product or service benefits customers uniquely.

- **Define Your Budget:** Allocate resources considering advertising, social media, or press releases based on affordability.

- **Determine Your Channels**: Select appropriate channels like blogs, social media, or paid ads based on your target audience.

- **Measure Success:** Establish metrics to evaluate the effectiveness of your marketing efforts in reaching and engaging your audience.

5.3. Benefits of Understanding Marketing Strategies

- **Competitive Advantage**: Marketing strategies seek to establish a sustainable competitive advantage by understanding consumer needs.

- **Communication Effectiveness:** The success of marketing assets, whether print ads or social media campaigns, is measured by their ability to convey the core value proposition.

- **Market Research Importance:** Market research is crucial for assessing campaign effectiveness, identifying untapped audiences, and aligning efforts with bottom-line goals.

- **Sales Boost:** Effective marketing strategies contribute to increased sales by targeting consumer needs and wants accurately.

5.4. Market Strategies in E-Commerce

In promoting a business, internet marketing strategies are often considered highly effective and budget-friendly for generating leads. Before implementing these strategies, it's crucial to understand each one; some are the following:

5.4.1. Digital Marketing

A digital marketing strategy for e-commerce outlines a plan to leverage online channels, such as organic search, social media, paid ads, and your website, to establish a robust internet presence and achieve specific marketing objectives. The primary aim is to enhance business visibility and attract new customers.

Differentiating between a digital marketing strategy and a campaign is crucial. While a strategy is a comprehensive plan for achieving digital goals, a campaign is a focused and time-bound initiative within that strategy. In essence, the strategy is the overarching plan, and campaigns are the tactical implementations to fulfill specific objectives.

Digital marketing campaign

A digital marketing campaign is a structured series of activities embedded within your broader digital marketing strategy, all working cohesively to achieve a particular objective. It serves as the operational unit that advances you toward a specific goal. For example, if your overarching digital marketing strategy aims to boost lead generation via social media, you might implement a campaign on Twitter. This campaign could involve sharing high-performing gated content to attract and generate more leads through the Twitter platform.

How to Create a Digital Marketing Strategy

- **Build Your Buyer Personas:**

The first step to the initiation of a robust digital marketing strategy is to build comprehensive buyer personas. These personas, representing your ideal customers, should be crafted through thorough research, surveys, and interviews.

Including quantitative data like location, age, income, and job title provides a solid foundation. It's imperative to base this information on real data to avoid assumptions that might lead your strategy astray. By understanding your audience's demographics, you can tailor your marketing efforts more effectively.

Next, align your marketing goals with the overall objectives of your business. Whether it's increasing online revenue or generating more leads through the website, clear and measurable goals are essential. Creating a high-level marketing plan that outlines priorities and identifies necessary digital marketing tools ensures a strategic approach.

Evaluate your existing digital channels and assets using the owned, earned, and paid media framework. Owned media comprises assets under your control, such as your website and social media profiles.

Earned media involves exposure gained through word-of-mouth marketing and positive reviews, while paid media includes channels where you invest for increased visibility. Categorizing your digital assets provides clarity and helps in decision-making.

Finally, conduct an audit of your owned media campaigns, which are predominantly content-driven. Content plays a pivotal role in converting visitors into leads and customers, improving online presence, and boosting organic traffic when optimized for search engines. Plan campaigns that align with your digital marketing goals, leveraging existing content and creating new pieces where necessary. This ensures a cohesive and effective approach to digital marketing.

- **Identify your goals and the digital marketing tools you'll need:**

Aligning your digital marketing goals with the overarching objectives of your business is crucial for success. Clearly defined and measurable goals provide direction and purpose to your marketing efforts. For instance, if your business aims to boost online revenue by 20%, your marketing team might set a goal of generating 50% more leads through the website compared to the previous year, contributing significantly to the overall success.

To streamline your approach, utilize a high-level marketing plan template. This template serves as a valuable tool to outline your annual marketing strategy, identify top priorities, and establish a comprehensive roadmap for achieving your goals. The template facilitates a structured and organized planning process, ensuring that each digital marketing initiative directly contributes to the larger business objectives.

- **Evaluate your existing digital channels and assets:**

When assessing your current digital marketing channels and assets for inclusion in your strategy, it's essential to take a holistic view to avoid feeling overwhelmed. Create a comprehensive spreadsheet to categorize each digital vehicle or asset into owned, earned, and paid media using the framework for a clear understanding.

Owned media represents the digital assets your brand owns entirely, such as your website, social media profiles, blog content, or imagery. This category includes off-site content you own, like blogs published on platforms such as Medium.

Earned media encompasses exposure gained through word-of-mouth marketing, including distributed content on external websites, PR efforts, and positive customer experiences. This recognition is earned through press mentions, positive reviews, and content sharing on social media.

Paid media involves channels or vehicles where you invest money to capture the attention of your target audience. Examples include Google Ads, paid social media posts, native advertising, or any medium where payment enhances visibility.

To illustrate the framework, consider a scenario where you have a valuable piece of owned content on a landing page. Integrating the framework involves making the content shareable to encourage audience distribution via social media, increasing traffic. Supporting its success may involve promoting the content on your Facebook page through paid visibility to the target audience.

This framework's synergy demonstrates how owned, earned, and paid media can work together for optimal results. Evaluate the most effective solution aligned with your goals, deciding which channels to incorporate into your digital marketing strategy. Keep track of paid media efforts using a free Paid Media Template to refine your strategy further.

- **Audit and plan your owned media campaigns:**

In the realm of digital marketing, owned media is, at the core, predominantly manifested as content. This encompasses a wide range of messages your brand disseminates, including the About

Us page, product descriptions, blog posts, eBooks, infographics, podcasts, and social media posts. Content plays a pivotal role in converting website visitors into leads and customers, concurrently enhancing your brand's online presence.

The integration of search engine optimization (SEO) principles into this content further amplifies its impact by boosting search visibility and organic traffic.

Regardless of your specific digital marketing strategy goal, incorporating owned content is essential. To commence this process, it is imperative to determine the type of content that will effectively contribute to achieving your goals.

For instance, if the objective is to generate 50% more leads via the website compared to the previous year, evaluate the historical performance of content, particularly focusing on pieces that have previously served as successful lead generators.

Here's a concise process to guide you in determining the owned content needed to align with your digital marketing strategy goals:

- **Assess Past Performance**

Review the performance of existing content, emphasizing pieces that have historically contributed to lead generation. Identify content that has proven to be effective in achieving similar goals.

- **Keyword Research**

Conduct thorough keyword research to identify relevant terms and phrases within your industry and audience. Strategically incorporate these keywords into your content to enhance search engine visibility.

- **Identify Content Gaps**

Pinpoint any gaps in your existing content that may hinder the achievement of your goals. Determine topics or areas that require new content to fill these gaps.

- **Content Calendar**

Develop a comprehensive content calendar outlining the creation and publication schedule for each piece of content. This ensures a structured and consistent approach to your owned media campaigns.

- **Diversify Content Formats**

Consider diversifying content formats to cater to diverse audience preferences. This could involve incorporating blog posts, videos, infographics, or interactive content to provide a well-rounded and engaging experience.

5.4.2. Search Engine Optimization

A search engine is like a digital librarian for the internet. When you enter a question or keywords (called a search query), the search engine scans its vast database of websites and creates a list of results.

The results are ranked based on how closely they match your query and other factors like popularity and credibility. The goal is to provide you with the most relevant and reliable information.

Popular search engines use complex algorithms to crawl constantly and index new content on the web. They make it easier for users to access a wide range of information quickly and efficiently.

SEO is like the art and science of making web pages show up higher when people search on Google or other search engines. When you search for something, you might see ads at the top – those are paid.

Below that are the regular results, and we call them "organic search results." Getting more people to visit a website through these regular results is what we call "organic search traffic." This is different from paid ads, which are often called search engine marketing (SEM) or pay-per-click (PPC). So, SEO helps your website be more visible in the regular results and brings in more visitors.

Process Of Search Engine Optimization

Search engines, like Google, employ intricate algorithms to determine which pages to display for specific queries. These algorithms consider numerous ranking factors to assess a page's quality. While the criteria are extensive, three fundamental metrics are pivotal in this evaluation:

- **Links:** The presence of links from other websites significantly influences a site's ranking. These links are akin to votes of quality, as reputable sites are more likely to link to high-quality content. The accumulation of such links enhances a site's authority, known as "PageRank" in Google's context.

- **Content:** Search engines scrutinize a webpage's content to gauge its relevance to user queries. An integral aspect of SEO involves crafting content tailored to keywords commonly searched by users. Aligning content with popular search terms enhances a page's visibility in search results.

- **Page Structure:** The structure of HTML code in webpages impacts a search engine's ability to assess them. SEO practices involve strategically placing relevant keywords in the title, URL, and headers of a page. Additionally, ensuring a site is easily crawlable contributes to improved SEO performance.

The SEO process revolves around optimizing these core components to secure higher rankings in search results. It encompasses actions such as acquiring quality links, creating targeted content, and structuring HTML code effectively to enhance a site's visibility and authority.

Some Main Search Engine Tools

SEO, a technical field, uses various tools and software to optimize websites. Some widely used tools are available for free, while others require payment.

- **Google Search Console:** This free tool by Google, formerly known as "Google Webmaster Tools," is a fundamental resource for SEO practitioners. It furnishes insights into keyword rankings and traffic reports and aids in identifying and resolving on-site technical issues.

- **Google Ads Keyword Planner:** Although primarily designed for paid search, this free Google tool is valuable for SEO. It offers keyword suggestions and search volume data, proving beneficial for effective keyword research.

- **Backlink Analysis Tools:** AHREFs and Majestic are prominent tools for analyzing backlinks. They enable users to scrutinize websites linking to their own or competitors' sites, aiding in the discovery of new links during the link-building process.

- SEO platforms, including Site Improve, Moz, Bright Edge, and Search metrics, offer essential tools for optimizing websites. These platforms assist in tracking keyword rankings, conducting keyword research, and identifying on-page and off-page SEO opportunities.

- Social Media: While most social media platforms may not directly impact SEO, they serve as valuable networking tools. Building relationships with other web admins through social media can lead to opportunities for link-building and guest posting.

5.4.3. Social Media Marketing

In the dynamic landscape of digital marketing, Social Media Marketing (SMM) stands out as a powerful strategy that has transformed the way businesses connect with their audience. This approach capitalizes on the ubiquitous presence of social media platforms to build brand awareness, engage customers, and drive business growth. Let's delve into the essence of Social Media Marketing and explore how businesses can harness its potential.

Understanding Social Media Marketing:

Social Media Marketing involves the use of social media platforms to connect with the target audience, build brand presence, and foster engagement. These platforms include popular names like Facebook, Instagram, Twitter, LinkedIn, and more. The primary goal is to create compelling content that resonates with the audience and encourages them to share it across their social networks, amplifying the brand's reach.

Benefits of social media for E-commerce

- **Expanded Reach:** Social media taps into a vast audience, allowing e-commerce retailers to connect with potential customers on platforms like Facebook, Twitter, and Instagram.

- **Targeted Engagement:** Engage users where they spend the most time online, offering a personalized approach distinct from traditional SEO and PPC campaigns.

- **Casual Communication:** Social media provides an informal channel for two-way communication, allowing businesses to engage with users interested in their products.

- **Viral Exposure:** The sharing nature of social media enables customers to introduce and share your brand, leading to organic exposure among extended networks.

Process of Social Media Marketing (SMM)

- **Define Objectives and Goals:** Clearly outline goals, such as brand awareness or lead generation, to guide your strategy.

- **Audience Research:** Understand your target audience through thorough research on demographics, interests, and online behavior.

- **Choose Relevant Platforms**: Select platforms aligning with your audience and business goals, considering varied demographics and content formats.

- **Create Engaging Content:** Craft compelling content, including images, videos, and infographics, fostering emotional connections through storytelling.

- **Content Calendar:** Develop a content calendar for consistent posting, ensuring a steady and diverse presence on social media.

- **Build a community**: Engage with your audience by responding to comments and messages, fostering a sense of community and loyalty.

- **Utilize Paid Advertising:** Explore paid advertising options for sponsored posts, targeted ads, and promoted content to reach specific demographics.

- **Analytics and Monitoring:** Regularly monitor performance metrics like engagement, reach, click-through rates, and conversions.

- **Adapt to Algorithm Changes:** Stay informed about algorithm changes on social media platforms and adjust your strategy accordingly.

- **Handle Negative Feedback:** Address both positive and negative feedback transparently and promptly, contributing to a positive brand reputation.

- **Evaluate and Adjust:** Regularly evaluate the effectiveness of your strategy, identifying areas for improvement and adjusting based on performance data.

- **Stay Informed and Evolve:** Stay informed about industry trends, emerging platforms, and changes in user behavior, evolving your strategy to stay relevant.

Top Four Social Media Platforms

1) Facebook:

- With nearly 1.5 billion active users, Facebook offers a massive audience.

- Create a dedicated business page to share product photos, sales announcements, and engaging content.

- Visual content performs exceptionally well, making it ideal for showcasing products.

- Utilize targeted ad campaigns to reach specific demographics based on age, gender, location, interests, and behaviors.

2) Twitter:

- Boasting 800 million users, Twitter is effective for e-commerce.

- 52% of users claim to have purchased a product they first saw on Twitter.

- It provides a platform for direct customer engagement and quick responses.

- Incorporate Twitter into your customer service strategy to build relationships and manage your online reputation.

3) Instagram:

- With 500 million monthly users, Instagram is a visual powerhouse.

- Showcase your products through visually appealing content.

- Share behind-the-scenes glimpses to connect with your audience on a personal level.

- Leverage Instagram's high engagement potential to build a loyal customer base.

4) Snapchat:

- Despite being relatively new for marketers, Snapchat is gaining traction.

- Boasting 150 million daily active users, it's particularly popular among the under-25 demographic.

- Use Snapchat to offer a behind-the-scenes look at your business and connect with a younger audience.

- Capitalize on the platform's novelty, as only 1% of marketers currently utilize it.

5.4.4. E-mail Marketing

Email marketing stands as a direct channel for businesses to communicate new products, sales, and updates directly to subscribers on their contact lists. This targeted approach, where subscribers willingly sign up for emails, enhances the likelihood of conversion compared to other channels.

With a proven high return on investment (ROI), email marketing is a crucial component of most businesses' inbound strategies.

Modern email marketing has evolved beyond generic mass mailings. It now emphasizes consent, segmentation, and personalization to engage target audiences more effectively. The focus is on understanding customer interests to foster long-term relationships.

While creating personalized campaigns might seem time-intensive, marketing automation and software play a significant role in streamlining these processes. In the end, a well-designed email marketing strategy not only drives sales but also contributes to building a community around your brand.

Benefits of E-mail Marketing

Email marketing serves as a vital tool in achieving key business objectives, offering benefits that contribute to sales growth, brand awareness, and customer loyalty.

Drive Sales:

- Email marketing campaigns can effectively boost sales by promoting special offers, discounts, or product launches.

- Techniques like sending coupons for birthdays/anniversaries, welcome emails, and abandoned cart reminders can further enhance conversions.

Increase Brand Awareness:

- Email provides a direct channel to reach individuals, fostering one-to-one communication with subscribers.

- Unlike social media, emails allow for curated and personalized content, making a more significant impact on brand awareness.

- Scalability in email marketing enables cost-effectively reaching a large audience compared to other channels.

Strengthen Customer Loyalty:

- Email plays a crucial role in nurturing leads, facilitating conversions, onboarding new customers, and retaining existing ones.

- Integration with Customer Relationship Management (CRM) systems streamlines communication, contributing to long-term customer loyalty.

The Process of your contact list for E-mail Marketing

Crafting effective marketing emails involves strategic planning and compelling content. Here's a concise guide to streamline your approach:

- **Define Your Strategy:** Clearly outline your email marketing goals, whether they are promoting a new product, sharing discounts, or updating subscribers on company news. Establish measurable objectives to guide your content creation.

- **Design Impactful Emails:** Utilize user-friendly drag-and-drop editors to design professional and visually appealing emails. Focus on simplicity, incorporating your brand elements, such as logos and visuals. Prioritize responsive templates for optimal viewing across devices.

- **Optimize Subject Line and Sender Details:** Craft a captivating subject line within 50 characters, highlighting the most enticing offer. Prioritize A/B testing for subject lines and avoid over-promotional language. Enhance sender trustworthiness by incorporating your brand name and maintaining consistency.

- **Leverage Preheader/Preview Text:** Optimize the preheader or preview text to complement the subject line, providing additional context. This snippet appears after the subject line, particularly on mobile devices. Aim for a cohesive narrative that intrigues the reader.

- **Write Persuasive Copy:** Tailor your email copy to offer value, align with audience interests, and embody your brand's tone. Address audience needs, maintain a conversational tone, and consider storytelling. Break up the copy with short paragraphs and use bullet points for clarity.

5.5.5 Content Marketing

Content marketing is the practice of creating and distributing valuable, relevant, and consistent content to engage a target audience. Unlike traditional advertising, it aims to provide information that genuinely interests and benefits the audience.

The primary goals of content marketing are to build trust, establish thought leadership, and drive profitable customer action. Instead of pushing promotional messages, the focus is on delivering value to the audience.

Blogging is highlighted as a prominent content marketing tactic. Despite some dissenting opinions, the passage argues that blogging remains crucial for businesses looking to attract customers who are genuinely interested in their products and services.

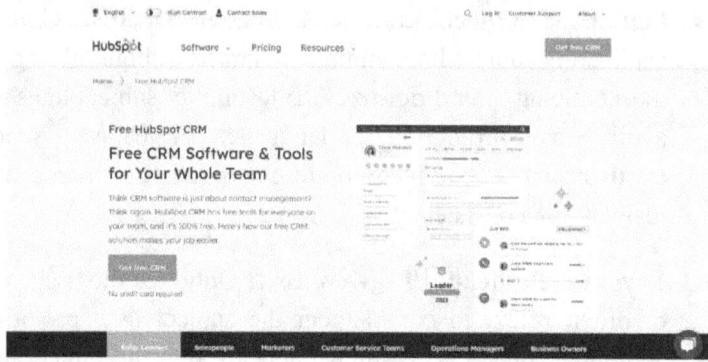

The example of HubSpot, a marketing software provider, is used to illustrate the effectiveness of blogging. Well-written and well-researched blog posts can address the urgent needs of potential customers. HubSpot's users, often marketing professionals, benefit from content that assists them in creating plans, campaigns, and editorial calendars.

The key message is to blog with a purpose, aiming to solve customer problems. Understanding the target audience and their pain points is crucial for creating highly targeted and genuinely helpful content. Overall, the passage advocates for strategic content marketing, particularly through blogging, to establish a meaningful connection with the audience and drive customer engagement.

Online Marketing Benefits of Content Marketing

- **Boosts Web Traffic:**

Regularly publishing fresh and relevant blog content has a positive impact on SEO rankings. This, in turn, attracts more organic visitors to your website. Additionally, sharing content on social media and other channels helps maintain engagement with your audience and enhances overall visibility.

- **Establishes Authority and Credibility:**

Sharing your expertise and insights through blog articles and other content positions both you and your company as thought leaders in your industry.

This not only builds trust with your audience but also establishes you as a reliable and knowledgeable resource. By addressing your audience's pain points, you demonstrate a deep understanding of their needs.

- **Generates Leads and Conversions:**

Creating engaging and relevant content attracts potential customers who are genuinely interested in your business. This content can guide them through the buyer's journey.

Moreover, incorporating Calls-to-Action (CTAs) in your content encourages readers to take specific actions, such as subscribing to a newsletter or registering for a free trial. This process helps convert readers into leads and, ultimately, into customers.

Process of Content Creation

The process of content creation involves several key steps to develop and produce high-quality, engaging content. Here's a breakdown of the content creation process:

Define Objectives and Audience:

- Clearly outline the objectives of the content. Whether it's to inform, entertain, or persuade, having a clear purpose is essential.

- Understand your target audience, their preferences, and the problems or questions they seek answers to.

Research and Ideation:

- Conduct thorough research on the chosen topic. Gather information from reliable sources to ensure the content is accurate and up-to-date.

- Brainstorm ideas and develop a content plan. Identify key points, supporting details, and potential visual elements.

Keyword Integration:

- If the content is intended for online visibility, conduct keyword research to identify relevant terms. Integrate these keywords naturally into the content to enhance search engine optimization (SEO).

Create an Outline:

- Develop a structured outline that organizes the content logically. This serves as a roadmap for the writing process, ensuring a coherent flow of information.

Write the First Draft:

- Begin writing the first draft based on the outlined structure. Focus on conveying the main message clearly and concisely.

- Don't worry about perfection during the first draft; the goal is to get ideas onto paper.

Edit and Revise:

- Review the first draft for clarity, coherence, and consistency. Edit for grammar, spelling, and punctuation errors.

- Consider the overall structure and flow, ensuring a smooth transition between sections.

Incorporate Visual Elements:

- Enhance the content by incorporating relevant visual elements such as images, infographics, or videos. Visuals can aid in understanding and engagement.

Add Value and Detail:

- Ensure the content provides value to the audience. Add specific details, examples, or statistics to support key points and make the content more informative.

Check SEO Elements:

- If applicable, ensure that SEO elements are optimized. This includes meta titles, meta descriptions, and the strategic placement of keywords within the content.

Finalize and Proofread:

- Finalize the content by proofreading it thoroughly. Check for any remaining errors and ensure that the content aligns with the established objectives.

Format for Readability:

- Format the content for easy readability. Use subheadings, bullet points, and short paragraphs to break up text and make it more digestible for readers.

Review for Consistency:

- Review the content to ensure consistency in tone, style, and messaging. This is especially important if multiple contributors are involved.

Seek Feedback:

- If possible, seek feedback from peers, colleagues, or target audience members. External perspectives can offer valuable insights for improvement.

Final Approval:

- Obtain final approval from relevant stakeholders before publishing or sharing the content.

Publish and Promote:

- Once approved, publish the content on the chosen platform(s). Promote it through appropriate channels, such as social media, email newsletters, or other relevant outlets.

5.5. Summary

A marketing strategy is a comprehensive plan aimed at achieving specific marketing goals. It evaluates a business's current strengths and weaknesses in relation to set objectives, incorporating key elements like the value proposition, brand messaging, and target demographics.

This strategic roadmap serves as a guide for reaching potential consumers and involves crucial components such as the four Ps of marketing: product, price, place, and promotion. A robust marketing strategy centers around a company's value proposition, effectively conveying its identity and reasons for customer patronage.

Creating an effective marketing strategy involves steps like identifying clear goals, understanding the ideal customer, crafting compelling messages, allocating resources, selecting appropriate channels, and establishing metrics for success. Understanding marketing strategies is beneficial as they contribute to a sustainable competitive advantage, enhance communication effectiveness, and underscore the importance of market research. Effective marketing strategies also boost sales by accurately targeting consumer needs.

In the context of e-commerce, digital marketing is an effective and budget-friendly strategy that leverages online channels like organic search, social media and paid ads to enhance visibility. Distinguishing between a digital marketing strategy and campaigns is vital, with campaigns being focused initiatives within the broader strategy. SEO plays a pivotal role in the digital landscape, optimizing web pages to show up higher in search results.

Social media marketing utilizes platforms like Facebook, Twitter, and Instagram to build brand awareness and engage customers. Email marketing serves as a direct channel for businesses to communicate with subscribers, offering benefits such as driving sales and increasing brand awareness.

Content marketing, emphasizing the creation and distribution of valuable content, aims to build trust and drive profitable customer action. Blogging, as a crucial tactic within content marketing, is highlighted for addressing the urgent needs of potential customers and advocating for strategic content marketing to establish a meaningful connection with the audience.

May I Ask For A Smaller Favor?

At the outset, thank you for taking the time to read this book. You could have chosen any other book, but you took mine, and I totally appreciate this.

I hope you got a few actionable insights that will have a positive impact on your business success.

Can I ask for 30 seconds more of your time?

I'd love it if you could leave a review about the book. Reviews may not matter to big-name authors, but they're a tremendous help for authors like me, who don't have much following. They help me to grow my readership by encouraging folks to take a chance on my book.

To put it straight – **reviews are the lifeblood of any author.**

Please leave your review by going to the paltform you got this book from. It will just take less than a minute of your time, but it will tremendously help me to reach out to more people, so please leave your review.

Thanks for your support of my book. And I'd love to see your review.

Full Book Summary

The first chapter introduces the world of E-Commerce in the e-century, emphasizing the pivotal role of the Internet and ICT in economic growth. Steve Jobs' quote sets the tone, highlighting the importance of understanding customer needs. The chapter explores the challenges of technical and management skills in the ICT domain, encouraging readers to leverage available resources for skill development.

The concept of E-Commerce, short for Electronics Commerce, is elucidated, emphasizing its role in reducing costs, improving quality, and expediting delivery. Various methods like EDI, email, and EFT facilitate paperless business information exchange. The essence of E-Commerce is leveraging the internet for efficient business transactions, covering procurement, order entry, payment authentication, and more.

E-commerce is categorized into B2B, B2C, and C2C segments, offering a diverse range of online business activities. The definitions of E-Commerce by different experts provide nuanced perspectives, emphasizing its scope beyond online shopping. The distinction between E-Commerce and E-Business is discussed, with debates around their interpretations and constraints.

Chapter 1 then delves into the functions of E-Commerce, highlighting daily activities like Search Engine Optimization (SEO), product selection, merchandising, customer service, and analytics monitoring. Practical tips for each function, such as emphasizing unique, relevant content and optimizing page titles, are provided to enhance readers' E-Commerce skills.

Opportunities and challenges in the Indian E-Commerce landscape are discussed. E-commerce is recognized as a crucial component of India's trade facilitation policy, with significant growth since economic reforms in 1991. Opportunities include global trade, virtual businesses, lower search costs, and round-the-clock transactions. Challenges encompass high return rates, reliance on cash on delivery, payment gateway failures, low internet penetration, feature phone dominance, non-standardized addresses, logistical issues, and overfunded competitors.

Chapter 1 concludes by exploring the future scope and growth of E-Commerce. Macroeconomic factors like rising disposable income, increased internet users, and demand for debit/credit cards are identified as drivers. Segment-specific factors, especially in the online travel segment, contribute to the industry's growth. The chapter sets the stage for a comprehensive understanding of the evolution of e-commerce, its challenges, and its prospects.

Moving on to the next aspect, the electronic business landscape is diverse, encompassing various models tailored to specific interactions between businesses and consumers on the Internet. The Business-to-Business (B2B) model facilitates transactions between companies, involving intermediaries and emphasizing relationship-building across different sectors such as supplier management, inventory management, distribution, channel management, and payment processes. B2B applications play a vital role in streamlining business operations and fostering collaborations.

In Chapter 2, we examine B2B models further reveal three central approaches: supplier-centric, buyer-centric, and intermediary-centric. Each approach caters to specific business dynamics, with companies like Intel and Cisco exemplifying the supplier-centric model and the U.S. government showcasing the buyer-centric model. While the B2B model offers advantages such as instant purchases, increased revenue, expanded company presence, and closer business relationships, it is not without its challenges, including a limited market, long purchase decision times, an inverted power structure, and a sales process requiring substantial face time.

In contrast, the Business-to-Consumer (B2C) model involves direct interactions between businesses and individual consumers. This model, often referred to as internet retailing or E-tailing, relies on heavy advertising, substantial investments in infrastructure, and a strong customer care service to attract and retain customers. B2C transactions encompass a range of products, and the consumer shopping procedure involves distinct steps from identifying requirements to completing the transaction and awaiting product delivery.

Ultimately, the B2B and B2C models represent integral components of the e-business ecosystem, each presenting unique opportunities and challenges in the dynamic world of electronic commerce.

Further, The e-commerce landscape is incredibly diverse, offering various models that cater to distinct interactions between businesses and consumers. The Business-to-Consumer (B2C) model stands out for its advantages on both consumer and business fronts. From the consumer perspective, online shopping provides unparalleled access to goods and services, potential cost savings, a wide variety of offerings, 24/7 shopping availability, a wide range of choices, and a hassle-free shopping experience. On the business side, B2C e-commerce brings lower transaction costs, access to global markets, cost-effective display of information, streamlined order processing, global market reach, and reduced overhead expenses.

However, challenges arise in the B2C realm, including intense competition, technology issues, catalog inflexibility, limited market reach, extended sales cycles, higher costs of doing business, and inefficient business administration processes. Consumers may face security concerns and encounter customer service challenges in the absence of face-to-face interactions.

The Consumer-to-Consumer (C2C) model, exemplified by platforms like eBay, offers consumers 24/7 availability, regularly updated websites, higher profitability through direct transactions, low transaction costs, and direct communication. Yet, it comes with disadvantages such as unsecured payments, potential scams and theft, and challenges in maintaining quality control.

The emerging Consumer-to-Business (C2B) model introduces a shift where individual consumers actively contribute to businesses, initiating direct contact and collaboration. Characterized by direct action, collaborative consumption, detailed segmentation, interaction, reciprocity, and bi-directionality, C2B represents a dynamic exchange that benefits both consumers and businesses.

In the dynamic landscape of e-commerce, each model presents unique opportunities and challenges, shaping the way businesses and consumers interact in the digital marketplace. The continued evolution of these models reflects the ongoing adaptation to changing consumer behaviors and technological advancements.

Delving deeper into the diverse landscape of e-commerce, we find that it is marked by a multitude of models, each shaped by technological advancements, changing consumer behaviors, and evolving business strategies. The emergence of the Consumer-to-Business (C2B) model stands out as a revolutionary shift driven by bidirectional network connectivity and decreased technology costs. This model allows individuals to actively engage with businesses, offering products, services, and innovative ideas.

The C2B model finds application in platforms like Google AdSense, Commission Junction, and Amazon's affiliate programs, where individuals contribute to advertising and selling services. Its advantages lie in its versatile description, graphical representation, centralized configuration, and integration with Java documentation, providing a comprehensive understanding and efficient management.

Beyond C2B, the e-commerce landscape extends to Business-to-Government (B2G) and Government-to-Business (G-to-B) interactions, showcasing the role of technology in facilitating transactions and collaborations between businesses and government entities. Other emerging models, such as Business-to-Peer Networks, Consumer-to-Government, and various Peer-to-Peer interactions, highlight the continued evolution and adaptation within the digital marketplace.

The Brokerage Model plays a pivotal role in connecting buyers and sellers across various market segments, exemplified by platforms like eBay. It leverages global reach, offering advantages over traditional offline brokerage. Additionally, the Value Chain Model emphasizes the sequence of activities involved in creating and delivering products, showcasing the importance of adding value at each stage.

Furthermore, the Advertising Model, M-commerce, and other emerging models like Consumer-to-Peer Networks and Government-to-Consumer demonstrate the dynamic nature of e-commerce, adapting to the growing influence of mobile technology and diverse business strategies.

In this ever-evolving landscape, the success of e-commerce relies on continuous innovation, efficient utilization of technology, and a deep understanding of consumer and business dynamics. As new models emerge and existing ones evolve, the future of e-commerce promises further transformation and integration into various aspects of our socio-economic ecosystem.

The third dimension to explore, venturing into the realm of online entrepreneurship, is undoubtedly an exhilarating journey but one that demands meticulous planning, strategic thinking, and continuous adaptation. The narrative of businesses hastily transitioning online during the COVID-19 pandemic serves as a cautionary tale, emphasizing that success in e-commerce is not just about creating a flashy website but rather about laying a solid foundation and sustaining momentum.

The planning phase, as discussed in **Chapter 3.1**, underscores the need for careful consideration of factors such as procurement processes, storage solutions, compelling content creation, efficient delivery systems, stock management, brand integration, and the synergy between physical and online stores. Each of these elements plays a pivotal role in establishing and maintaining a successful e-commerce venture.

Navigating potential pitfalls, as outlined in **Chapter 3.1.2,** involves aligning existing resources with e-commerce plans, comprehending the intricacies of different business models, and gaining insight into the true costs involved. Understanding these challenges ensures a smooth and strategic transition to online sales, preventing unforeseen obstacles that might hinder the growth of the business.

Setting objectives, as explored in **Chapter 3.1.3,** involves making crucial decisions about manufacturing and drop shipping and understanding the emotional and risk dynamics associated with each approach. Uncovering opportunities, as detailed in **Chapter 3.1.4,** emphasizes competitor analysis, staying abreast of industry trends, and employing social listening to remain vigilant and responsive to market dynamics.

As the journey progresses into setting up the e-commerce store, **Chapter 3.2** provides insights into the key elements of a successful online presence, including website components and popular e-commerce platforms like Shopify. The conclusion is clear: success in the dynamic world of e-commerce requires a holistic approach, careful planning, and a continuous commitment to understanding and meeting customer needs in an ever-evolving digital landscape. The adventure is exciting, but success lies in the details, strategies, and adaptability woven into the fabric of the online entrepreneurial journey.

In the rapidly evolving landscape of e-commerce, the journey from establishing an online store to ensuring seamless transactions and efficient logistics is a multifaceted adventure. The various platforms available, such as WooCommerce, Wix, BigCommerce, and OpenCart, present entrepreneurs with a spectrum of choices, each tailored to specific needs and preferences.

WooCommerce, deeply integrated into the WordPress ecosystem, epitomizes open-source brilliance. Its cost-effectiveness, coupled with extensive customization options, empowers businesses to create unique online storefronts. The user-friendly dynamics inherited from WordPress ensure a smooth onboarding experience and mobile optimization and SEO tools enhance visibility in the competitive digital landscape. With a community-backed support system, WooCommerce becomes more than just a platform; it becomes a collaborative environment for growth. Its content marketing prowess, aligned with WordPress capabilities, elevates it as an ideal choice for those aiming to bolster their brand's online presence. The seamless integration with various payment gateways further solidifies WooCommerce's position as a robust e-commerce solution.

Wix, on the other hand, emerges as a user-friendly launchpad for beginners entering the global e-commerce arena. Its simplicity in design and affordability, with pricing ranging from $17 to $25 per month, caters to budget-conscious entrepreneurs. The intuitive drag-and-drop interface facilitates the effortless creation of visually appealing and functional online spaces. The platform's versatile widgets and a plethora of templates provide aesthetic diversity, allowing businesses to align their online presence with brand identity. Wix's gateway integration harmony ensures a hassle-free transaction process, contributing to a positive online shopping experience.

BigCommerce, renowned for scalability, is tailored for growing ventures. Its user-friendly features, responsive templates, robust inventory system, and built-in SEO tools position it as a comprehensive solution for businesses of varying sizes. OpenCart, an open-source platform, offers flexibility and adaptability without requiring extensive technical expertise. Its straightforward setup and range of extensions cater to diverse e-commerce needs.

As small businesses venture into the digital marketplace, the decision to build an online store becomes a strategic move for growth. The internet not only expands sales to a broader audience but also levels the playing field against larger competitors. Understanding the suitability of products for e-commerce involves considerations such as product comprehension, profitability, digital delivery feasibility, and geographic appeal. These guidelines assist businesses in determining whether their offerings align with the dynamics of online selling.

Building an online presence involves crucial steps like registering a domain, building a site, and facilitating secure online payments. Platforms like Wix, Shopify, and WooCommerce offer flexibility in this journey. Whether businesses opt for a do-it-yourself approach or hire a web designer/developer, selecting a reliable hosting service is essential for seamless operations.

Setting up secure online payments involves obtaining a merchant account and a payment gateway account. Understanding the credit card payment flow, from authorization to settlement/funding, ensures a smooth and secure transaction experience for customers.

Promoting the online store is paramount for visibility and customer attraction. Search engine optimization (SEO), link building, and pay-per-click advertising enhance online visibility. Leveraging social media, email marketing, and integrating web presence into offline marketing strategies contribute to a comprehensive promotional approach.

Authorize.Net's security services, including the Advanced Fraud Detection Suite™, Comodo SSL Certificates, and integration with

FreshBooks, further enhance the safety and efficiency of online transactions.

In the logistics and fulfillment phase, the order processing workflow, inventory management, packing and shipping, order tracking, and delivery confirmation play pivotal roles. Selecting appropriate shipping partners, optimizing packaging for sustainability, and addressing international shipping challenges contribute to the overall success of the e-commerce venture. Returns and exchanges, when handled transparently, become opportunities to showcase excellent customer service.

Continuous improvement in logistics involves gathering customer feedback, analyzing performance analytics, and refining processes. This ongoing commitment to enhancement ensures that the e-commerce production continues to impress, leaving the audience – the customers – with a standing ovation.

In conclusion, the world of e-commerce offers a myriad of opportunities for businesses to thrive. From choosing the right platform to building a robust online presence, facilitating secure transactions, and optimizing logistics, each step contributes to the success of the grand production. As businesses embrace the digital frontier, the backstage crew of logistics and fulfillment plays a crucial role in ensuring a seamless and memorable experience for customers, ultimately earning the coveted standing ovation in the competitive world of online commerce.

In the ever-changing terrain of the contemporary digital sphere, businesses are increasingly acknowledging the transformative prowess of e-marketing, establishing it as a cornerstone in their strategic endeavors. Referred to interchangeably as electronic marketing, online marketing, or internet marketing, this dynamic approach emerges as an indispensable tool, elevating online visibility and fostering meaningful connections with target audiences. The landscape of e-marketing fundamentally alters the traditional paradigms of product promotion and consumer engagement, seamlessly weaving together information management, public relations, customer services, and sales under its expansive purview. Positioned as a linchpin within the broader scope of electronic commerce, e-marketing assumes a pivotal role, intricately shaping the dynamics of contemporary business interactions.

E-marketing, synonymous with Internet Marketing and Online Marketing, involves leveraging the Internet to promote products or services. This comprehensive approach reaches the target audience through various channels, including smartphones, devices, social media, email, and wireless media. Integrated into the broader framework of integrated marketing communications (IMC), e-marketing has become an indispensable component for brands seeking growth across diverse digital platforms.

The meaning and definition of e-marketing encompass conducting marketing activities and achieving objectives through electronic mediums. This involves utilizing computer systems, the internet, and other electronic networks to exchange goods or services, with their values determined in terms of price. Cisco specialists highlight that e-marketing includes all activities conducted through the Internet to attract, win, and retain customers. It enhances traditional marketing functions by incorporating strategies like email campaigns, banner ads, referrals, and video ads to attract and retain customers.

E-marketing is not merely a promotional tool; it is a strategic approach that combines cost-effectiveness, comprehensive product presentation, market understanding, and continuous customer engagement to build enduring relationships and drive sustained business success. It complements traditional marketing methods, and its flexible and cost-effective nature makes it suitable for both large enterprises and small firms, contributing to significant results in various business contexts.

The importance of e-marketing lies in its ability to promote sales consistently, unbound by specific dates or times. It offers flexibility in advertising products at any given moment, widening the reach to a diverse customer base and fostering enduring customer relationships. Overcoming geographical limitations is another key advantage, as e-marketing enables businesses to connect with customers in remote areas without the constraints of distance. It is cost-effective, eliminating substantial expenses associated with physical stores and appealing to investors. Moreover, e-marketing excels in providing detailed product explanations and specifications, enhancing purchase likelihood by tailoring product profiles to diverse customer segments.

The benefits of e-marketing extend to both businesses and consumers. Consumers benefit from accessible product information, streamlined purchasing processes with convenient payment options, and the expansive reach of the internet that provides access to a global marketplace. For businesses, e-marketing offers scalability by eliminating spatial constraints associated with traditional marketing, resulting in cost efficiency and competitive pricing. Overall, e-marketing revolutionizes the consumer experience, redefining the landscape of modern commerce by empowering individuals with information, convenience, global accessibility, product variety, and cost savings.

However, businesses need help navigating the dynamic realm of e-marketing. Staying on top of trends, facing intense competition, setting appropriate budgets, and managing data efficiently are among the key challenges. Strategies to overcome these challenges involve adopting a targeted approach to trends aligned with industry specifics, conducting comprehensive competitor analyses, allocating budgets based on revenue and industry benchmarks, and investing in data management software for streamlined tracking and analysis.

E-marketing has emerged as an indispensable force in the digital era, reshaping how businesses connect with consumers and promote their products. Its strategic approach, combined with the myriad benefits it offers, positions e-marketing as a key driver of enduring customer relationships and sustained business success in the competitive landscape of the digital marketplace.

In navigating the complexities of the digital marketing landscape, businesses encounter an array of challenges that demand strategic solutions. The evolving nature of consumer behavior, technological advancements, and the competitive digital space necessitate a proactive approach to address these hurdles. Here, we delve into the concluding insights on overcoming the challenges posed by e-marketing and how businesses can ensure sustained success in the dynamic realm of digital marketing.

Generating quality leads remains a persistent challenge in e-marketing. The task requires precision in targeting and fostering genuine interest among potential customers. The creation of detailed buyer personas, rooted in real customer profiles and enriched with demographic details, serves as a fundamental strategy. These personas act as guiding beacons, ensuring that marketing efforts resonate authentically with the intended audience.

Another challenge lies in finding the right marketing tools amid a plethora of options. The abundance of tools, ranging from email management to customer data processing, necessitates careful consideration. Third-party resources like G2.com, which offer unbiased analyses and seek recommendations from professional networks, are effective solutions. These approaches empower businesses to make informed decisions and select tools tailored to their specific needs.

Adaptability emerges as a crucial factor in e-marketing success. The challenge lies in overcoming the reluctance to embrace change and explore new strategies. Allocating a portion of the marketing budget to explore new channels and continuously reviewing existing channels for reallocation based on performance fosters an adaptable mindset. Striking a balance between proven strategies and the exploration of new opportunities is essential for sustained growth.

Influencer collaboration, though a powerful strategy, presents its own set of challenges. Identifying and collaborating with the right influencers requires thorough research and alignment of values with the brand. Utilizing influencer marketing platforms or agencies streamlines the process, ensuring authenticity in partnerships and maximizing the impact of influencer collaborations.

Measuring return on investment (ROI) poses a complex challenge, especially with multiple channels and varied metrics. Implementing tracking tools and analytics platforms and setting specific goals tied to measurable outcomes are crucial steps. Regular evaluation and adjustment of strategies based on data insights optimize ROI and enhance the overall effectiveness of marketing campaigns.

Creating quality content, a time-consuming task is a challenge for businesses with limited time and multiple projects. Addressing this challenge involves effective time management through content calendars and breaking down the content creation process into manageable steps. Alternatively, outsourcing content creation to specialized agencies provides relief, ensuring the delivery of high-quality content.

Identifying and entering new markets introduces complexities related to market analysis and competition. Studying competitors' market expansion strategies and implementing proven marketing strategies tailored to the new market's dynamics help refine and optimize the approach.

Testing new channels poses challenges due to the learning curve associated with unfamiliar platforms. Thorough research, leveraging industry expertise, and seeking guidance from experts or marketing companies with diverse channel experience are key solutions to navigate the challenges of testing new avenues.

Crisis management and globalization challenges round out the spectrum of e-marketing hurdles. Developing a crisis management plan, monitoring channels for early signs of issues, and acting transparently and promptly is vital for handling unexpected crises. Expanding globally requires thorough market research, tailoring strategies to local cultures, and leveraging translation services and local experts for effective communication.

Employee training and engagement are critical for ensuring that marketing teams stay abreast of evolving technologies and strategies. Continuous training programs, a collaborative work culture, and opportunities for professional development contribute to a skilled and engaged marketing workforce.

Pivoting towards e-marketing success hinges on a strategic approach to overcome these challenges. Businesses that embrace adaptability, invest in comprehensive research, leverage technology, and foster a culture of continuous improvement will thrive in the ever-evolving landscape of digital marketing. By addressing these challenges strategically, businesses can enhance their marketing effectiveness and ensure sustained success in the dynamic digital landscape.

In Chapter 5, we discussed that a robust marketing strategy serves as the compass guiding businesses toward achieving specific goals. It involves a comprehensive assessment of a company's current strengths and weaknesses, outlining tactics to meet objectives effectively. Essential components of a marketing strategy include the value proposition, brand messaging, and target customer demographics, encapsulating the four Ps of marketing: product, price, place, and promotion. This strategic roadmap becomes a focal point for reaching potential consumers, converting them into customers, and ultimately paving the way for business success.

Understanding marketing strategies is pivotal for any business aiming to navigate the competitive landscape effectively. A well-crafted strategy centers around a company's value proposition, shaping its identity and operational principles. This becomes a guiding template for marketing initiatives across all products and services. For instance, retail giant Walmart is synonymous with a commitment to "everyday low prices," dictating its business operations and marketing endeavors.

Creating a marketing strategy involves a systematic approach. It begins with identifying goals, understanding the target audience, crafting compelling messages, allocating budget resources, choosing appropriate channels, and establishing metrics to measure success. This structured process ensures that marketing efforts are aligned with broader business objectives and resonate effectively with the intended audience.

The benefits of understanding marketing strategies are multifaceted. A well-defined strategy creates a sustainable competitive advantage by addressing consumer needs, enhances communication effectiveness through a clear value proposition, and underscores the importance of market research in aligning efforts with bottom-line goals. Moreover, effective marketing strategies contribute to increased sales by accurately targeting consumer needs and wants.

In the realm of e-commerce, internet marketing strategies play a crucial role in promoting businesses effectively. Digital marketing, a cornerstone of e-commerce strategies, involves leveraging online channels such as organic search, social media, paid ads, and websites to establish a robust internet presence and achieve specific marketing objectives. Distinguishing between a digital marketing strategy and a campaign is essential, with the former being a comprehensive plan and the latter a focused, time-bound initiative within that plan.

Search Engine Optimization (SEO) is a key component of digital marketing, aiming to enhance a website's visibility in organic search results. The SEO process involves optimizing factors such as links, content, and page structure to secure higher rankings. Various tools like Google Search Console, Google Ads Keyword Planner, and backlink analysis tools aid in optimizing websites effectively.

Social Media Marketing (SMM) stands out as a powerful strategy in the digital marketing landscape, transforming the way businesses connect with their audience. It involves using social media platforms to build brand awareness, engage customers, and drive business growth. The process includes defining objectives and goals, audience research, choosing relevant platforms, creating engaging content, building a community, utilizing paid advertising, and monitoring analytics.

Email marketing remains a direct and effective channel for businesses to communicate with subscribers. Evolving beyond generic mass mailings, modern email marketing emphasizes consent, segmentation, and personalization. Marketing automation and software streamline these processes, making them a vital component of businesses' inbound strategies.

In essence, a comprehensive understanding of marketing strategies, both traditional and digital, is imperative for businesses seeking sustained success in a dynamic and competitive landscape. By aligning marketing efforts with overarching business goals, effectively utilizing digital channels, and staying attuned to evolving consumer behaviors, businesses can thrive and navigate the ever-changing terrain of the market.

Nearing the end of our analysis, the comprehensive exploration of marketing strategies, encompassing traditional and digital realms, highlights their pivotal role in steering businesses toward success. A well-crafted marketing strategy is not merely a set of tactics. Still, a guiding roadmap that evaluates a business's strengths and weaknesses aligns with objectives and provides a focused approach to achieving success. It is the backbone that shapes a company's identity, communicates its value proposition, and navigates the competitive landscape.

Understanding marketing strategies is crucial as they offer a range of benefits. They create a sustainable competitive advantage by accurately addressing consumer needs, enhancing communication effectiveness through clear value propositions, and emphasizing the importance of market research in aligning efforts with business goals. Moreover, effective marketing strategies contribute significantly to increased sales by precisely targeting consumer needs and wants.

In the dynamic world of e-commerce, digital marketing emerges as a cost-effective and impactful strategy. Distinguishing between a comprehensive digital marketing strategy and focused campaigns is vital for success. The role of SEO in optimizing web visibility and the power of social media in building brand awareness are pivotal components. Email marketing, as a direct communication channel, stands out for its ability to drive sales and increase brand awareness, particularly when integrated with Customer Relationship Management (CRM) systems.

Content marketing, as a practice of creating and distributing valuable content, adds a layer of depth to marketing strategies. The focus is on building trust, establishing thought leadership, and driving profitable customer action. Blogging, a prominent tactic within content marketing, remains relevant and effective, as exemplified by HubSpot's success in addressing the urgent needs of its audience.

The benefits of content marketing extend to boosting web traffic, establishing authority and credibility, and generating leads and conversions. The content creation process involves defining objectives and audience, thorough research, keyword integration, creating a structured outline, writing drafts, editing, incorporating visual elements, adding value and detail, checking SEO elements, finalizing, proofreading, formatting for readability, and seeking feedback. This comprehensive process ensures that the content aligns with objectives, is accurate and engaging, and resonates with the target audience.

In essence, a successful marketing strategy is a multifaceted approach that integrates traditional and digital channels, considering the specific needs and preferences of the target audience. It involves understanding the overarching goals of the business, crafting compelling messages, and strategically selecting channels that resonate with the audience. The synergy of these elements contributes to a holistic and effective marketing strategy.

As businesses continue to navigate the complexities of the market, staying attuned to emerging trends, evolving consumer behaviors, and technological advancements is essential. Adapting marketing strategies to align with these changes ensures relevance and sustained success. In this ever-changing landscape, the strategic fusion of traditional principles and digital innovations is the key to unlocking new opportunities and maintaining a competitive edge.

To conclude this section, a well-defined and executed marketing strategy is not a one-time effort but an ongoing process that requires agility, adaptability, and a deep understanding of the evolving dynamics of the business environment. As businesses strive for growth and market leadership, the foundation of a robust marketing strategy remains indispensable, guiding them through the intricacies of a rapidly changing landscape and steering them toward sustained success.

COULD YOU PLEASE LEAVE A REVIEW ON THE BOOK?

One Last Time!

I'd love it if you could leave a review about the book. Reviews may not matter to big-name authors, but they are a tremendous help for authors like me, who don't have much following. They help me to grow my readership by encouraging folks to take a chance on my books.

To put it straight- **reviews are the lifeblood of any author.**

Please leave your review by going to the paltform you got this book from. It will just take less than a minute of your time, but it will tremendously help me to reach out to more people, so please leave your review.

It will just take less than a minute of yours, but it will tremendously help me to reach out to more people, so please leave your review.

Thank you for supporting my work, and I'd love to see your review of the book.

REFERENCE

- Joseph P.T., E-Commerce – An Indian Perspective
- https://search.app/BCbzm7UoieARKVow8
- https://backup.pondiuni.edu.in/storage/dde/dde_ug_pg_books/E-%20Commerce.pdf
- https://nou.edu.ng/coursewarecontent/CIT%20415%20FINAL.pdf
- https://digitalmarketinginstitute.com/blog/how-to-set-up-an-ecommerce-business#
- https://www.dynamicpixel.co.in/blog/what-is-the-process-of-the-e-content-creation-process/
- https://www.prismglobalmarketing.com/blog/8-critical-components-develop-successful-online-marketing-plan
- https://coschedule.com/marketing-strategy#13-types-of-marketing-strategies
- https://www.investopedia.com/terms/m/marketing-strategy.asp
- https://neilpatel.com/blog/social-media-ecommerce/
- https://www.webfx.com/industries/retail-ecommerce/ecommerce/social-media/#:~:text=Ecommerce%20social%20media%20is%20the,profile%2C%20and%20products%20shared%20online
- https://www.webfx.com/blog/marketing/top-marketing-challenges/
- https://blog.hubspot.com/marketing/digital-strategy-guide
- https://peepstrategy.com/a-comprehensive-guide-to-the-buying-process-steps/
- https://directorist.com/blog/best-classified-ads-websites/
- https://www.waltervoronovic.com/glossary/what-is-b2g-e-commerce-explained/
- https://www.sayonetech.com/blog/ecommerce-ux/

www.ingramcontent.com/pod-product-compliance
Lightning Source LLC
Chambersburg PA
CBHW070923290526
45795CB00001B/401